ARE WE REALLY BETTER TOGETHER?

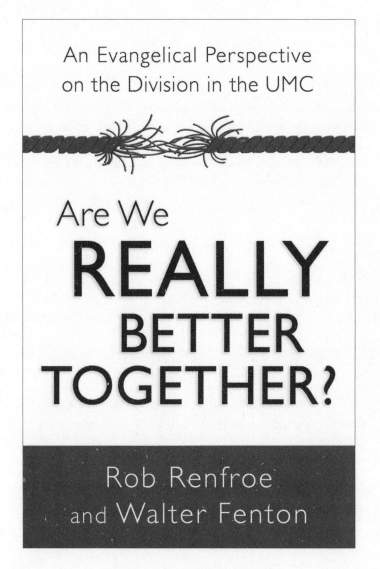

An Evangelical Perspective
on the Division in the UMC

Are We
REALLY
BETTER
TOGETHER?

Rob Renfroe
and Walter Fenton

Abingdon Press / Nashville

ARE WE REALLY BETTER TOGETHER?
AN EVANGELICAL PERSPECTIVE ON THE DIVISION IN THE UMC

ISBN 978-1-5018-63851

18 19 20 21 22 23 24 25 26 27 — 10 9 8 7 6 5 4 3 2 1
MANUFACTURED IN THE UNITED STATES OF AMERICA

CONTENTS

PREFACE

We will make no attempt in this slim volume to exhaustively rehearse the various arguments that have been marshaled for and against The United Methodist Church's sexual ethics, its teachings on marriage, and its ordination standards. The church's positions on these matters are not substantially different from the historic positions of the Roman Catholic Church, the Eastern Orthodox Church, and the vast majority of Protestant Christians worldwide. For at least the past fifty years, The United Methodist Church and other communities of faith have intensively studied these matters, prepared major statements, and revised or reaffirmed their teachings accordingly. In addition to this body of work, biblical scholars, Christian ethicists, theologians, Christian counselors, therapists, medical doctors, and geneticists have addressed the issues from a variety of perspectives,[1] so there is no need here to revisit all the arguments in detail.

To its credit, The United Methodist Church first engaged these matters almost fifty years ago, before it became more widely acceptable to do so in broader US culture. Furthermore, the statement the church adopted at its 1972 General Conference was carefully crafted, and many United Methodists still regard it as a gracious one, although others vehemently disagree. Eschewing inflammatory words like *sin* or *abomination*, the clear majority of the approximately one thousand delegates at the 1972 conference believed the following represented what the church already taught implicitly and what it should teach officially going forward: "we do not condone the practice of homosexuality and consider this practice *incompatible* with Christian teaching" (emphasis added).[2]

Clearly, the church was trying hard to make a very important distinction. It is not opposed to people who experience same-sex attraction or those who identify themselves as gay or lesbian. These people, no less than others, says the church, "are individuals of sacred worth, created in the image of God."[3] However, the church also wanted to make clear that it finds the *practice* of same-sex intimacy to be *incompatible* with Christian teaching. So to be perfectly clear, The United Methodist Church does not teach that people who experience same-sex attraction or identify themselves as LGBTQ+ are themselves incompatible with Christian teaching. The church only teaches that the *practice* is. It adamantly opposes the idea that people are, in and of themselves, incompatible when it comes to God's grace and love.

To be sure, LGBTQ+ people and their advocates would argue there is no real difference between the desire and the practice of sexual intimacy; the practice, they maintain, is part and parcel of an LGBTQ+ person's identity. Forbidding LGBTQ+ people from engaging in acts of sexual intimacy, they claim, is unjust, harmful, and even cruel, no matter how hard the church tries to differentiate the person from the practice. Consequently, it is not unusual to hear some LGBTQ+ advocates claim The United Methodist Church finds LGBTQ+ people incompatible. We of course do not believe this is the case, but we understand how LGBTQ+ advocates arrive at their justification for making the claim.

The United Methodist Church, in regular reaffirmations of its teaching, has repeatedly resisted this line of argument. It continues to claim the practice is incompatible with Scripture and two thousand years of Christian teaching. Furthermore, it maintains the cross of Christ can transform us, and the Holy Spirit working in and through us can empower us to surmount our sinful desires and enable us to conform our lives to Christian teachings. This is the life of Christian discipleship, and while no serious person claims it is easy, it is our call as Christ's followers.

Over the past fifty years, people in different faith communions have discovered there is little or no room for compromise between those who support Christianity's traditional sexual ethics and teachings on marriage and those who do not. For a time, the debate opened up a much-needed conversation regarding marriage and human sexuality in general. As a result of this conversation, we join others calling for the church to address with more intentionality sexual and marital brokenness in their many manifestations. We also readily acknowledge pastors are far more likely to be confronted with cases of infidelity in heterosexual marriage or serial divorce than with a person struggling and sometimes failing to resist a predisposition to same-sex intimacy. We believe pastors and teachers must gracefully and candidly preach and teach about the church's sexual ethics and its understanding of marriage. But having said that, we recognize that in recent years, opinions regarding the practice of homosexuality have only hardened. Conversations have often turned acrimonious, and the likelihood of people changing their minds—one way or another—has seriously diminished.

We should not assume, however, that this state of affairs is evidence of an unwillingness to enter into dialogue or to hear other people share their experiences. We believe it is possible, in fact likely, that people engaged in the debates over the church's sexual ethics, teachings on marriage, and ordination standards have simply reached firm conclusions regarding these matters. After fifty years of listening to each other, we understand each other's positions and reasons for holding them. So, further conversation, therefore, seldom produces new insights or changed minds. At best, such encounters end with people agreeing to disagree, or at worst, they end in mutual bewilderment and the suspicion that one's conversation partner is being obstinate. In short, more often than not, people on either side of the debate regard further conversation as fruitless and potentially harmful.

It is helpful to remember that the people of the church have reached this point with respect to a number of theological and ethical issues over the centuries. Sometimes they handled their disagreements well and other times not so well. Whatever the issue, over time they learned that while they could no longer live in the same communion or denomination, they could celebrate and promote those theological and ethical convictions they share in common. For example, Baptists do not baptize infants, and Methodists do. Baptists have their reasons for not doing so, just as Methodists have their reasons for doing so. Most Baptists and Methodists recognize that beyond gaining some mutual understanding for how each tradition arrives at its decision, there is not much point in arguing over the matter. Both parties are settled in their convictions and there is little likelihood either will change their minds. This does not mean both are right or that the question of infant baptism is unimportant. It simply means the parties have decided it is best for them to agree to disagree, to walk apart, and yet still join forces in those many other areas where there is mutual agreement.

Therefore, this book is not, at least first and foremost, an attempt to persuade those who oppose the church's teachings to change their minds. We believe, after fifty years of debate, there is little likelihood we will persuade people who oppose the church's teachings to change their minds. And likewise, it is unlikely opponents will change the minds of people who support the church's teachings. We will state briefly in the chapters that follow why we believe the United Methodist position is biblical and balanced, because we believe it's important to do so. But the primary question we want to address is how we move forward into the future. Are United Methodists, at this point in the long and contentious debate, really better together? Or is it time to find another way forward?

One last preliminary thought: Why "an *evangelical* perspective"? Choosing the best term to describe ourselves and others like us was challenging. Of late, the term *evangelical* has come to carry some rather negative baggage. For some, *evangelical* is now as much a political term as a theological one. It is assumed by some that it equals the "hard right" or worse. Others think of *evangelical* as a synonym for *fundamentalist* (anyone willing to invest the time will soon discover it is not).

The classical definition of an evangelical is one who warmly embraces Jesus Christ as Lord and Savior and joyfully shares that good news with others in both word and deed. Furthermore, an evangelical has a high view of the Bible. He or she believes it is

God-inspired and teaches everything necessary for understanding how God redeems us through Jesus' death on the cross and liberates us from our slavery to sin. The Bible is also an evangelical's sure guide for how to practice one's faith and conduct oneself both corporately and personally. And finally, most evangelicals readily ascribe to the great affirmations of the Apostles' and Nicene Creeds. Given this classical definition, we are happy and humbled to refer to ourselves as evangelicals.

Having said that, we also believe we are thoroughly orthodox Christians and warm-hearted Wesleyans, and we stand at the very center of The United Methodist Church. However, we recognize some people bristle when we use the term *orthodox*, *Wesleyan*, or *centrist* to describe ourselves. They believe we are appropriating such terms in a way that excludes others. So in light of the foregoing and for the purpose of Abingdon's Faultlines collection, we are honored to offer an *evangelical* perspective.[4]

1

WE ARE DIVIDED

The United Methodist Church is at a crossroads. We are a divided church, and the truth is, we are a hurting church.

Some believe our differences are so great and the ongoing battle so destructive that it is time to part ways. For over four decades, conservative and progressive United Methodists have expended enormous emotional, financial, and spiritual resources to gain the upper hand in a denomination that has declined every year since its founding in 1968. Surely our efforts and our finances would be better devoted to evangelism, discipleship, and missions. For the sake of the lost and the poor, shouldn't we set each other free to pursue what we see as God's calling upon our lives and our ministries?

Others believe we must do all we can to remain united. Those who champion this view do so because of the unity that Christ prayed for in John 17. They contend unity makes us a more effective church and therefore more likely to fulfill our mission of making "disciples of Jesus Christ for the transformation of the world."[1] We are better together, they claim. But, of course, that begs the question: Are we really together?

It is our contention we are not—and not simply because we have different views regarding sexuality and marriage. Our differences go deeper, to some of the foundational questions of what it means to be the church: Is Jesus Christ the only way to God? Is his death on the cross the only means for salvation? Are the Scriptures fully inspired and authoritative for revealing God's will and binding on how we should live? We believe the answer to these questions is a resounding Yes! while others in the church would answer differently. The painful truth is that we cannot agree on these central matters of our faith.

When a United Methodist bishop writes that we must not make an idol out of Jesus—the definition of an idol being "a false god"—while others believe Jesus is "very God of very God," are we together?

When a professor at one of our United Methodist seminaries teaches that other religious figures bring the same light to their followers as Jesus brings into the world, while others believe Jesus is utterly unique—the way and the truth and the life—are we together?

When one of our bishops encourages his churches to pray that we "take the next faithful step forward not based on . . . doctrine, tradition, or theology; judgments, fears, or convictions," and many of us believe that it's our theology and doctrine that tell us what it means to be faithful—are we really together?[2]

Many also recognize there are profound differences in the way we approach the Bible. More than a few laypersons would be surprised to learn many pastors and bishops would align themselves with the approach of Rev. Adam Hamilton, the founding pastor of Church of the Resurrection (Leawood, Kansas), when it comes to biblical interpretation. Hamilton has proposed what might be called a "three buckets" approach (he calls his three categories buckets): (1) some parts of the Bible were never actually true expressions of God's will, so they do not apply to us, because they reflect only the time and place in which they were written; (2) other parts were true expressions of God's will at one time, but no longer are, so they do not speak to our current context because God's will for us has changed; and finally, (3) there are those parts of the Bible that were true, still are, and always will be.[3] This interpretive strategy is foreign to Wesleyanism and to orthodox Christian teaching in general. Others believe, ourselves included, along with the Apostle Paul that "all Scripture is God-breathed and is useful for teaching, rebuking, correcting and training in righteousness" (2 Timothy 3:16). We are profoundly uncomfortable with the idea that certain parts of the Bible can be discarded because, contrary to what the church has believed for two thousand years, we who live in and have been influenced by a postmodern culture now know better. When we do not agree on the inspiration and authority of God's word—are we really together?

The inspiration of the Bible. The divinity of Christ. How we are saved from our sins. How we determine God's will for our lives and for the church. These are not small matters. They strike to the core of what it means to be Christian. If United Methodists are not together on these foundational issues—and we're not—can we really claim that we are together as a church?

The United Methodist Church in general has been able to overlook some of these differences because we do not vote on them at General Conference. And many pastors are careful not to reveal to their congregations their less than orthodox beliefs. They know the uproar it would create if they were open and honest about their views. As progressive pastor Rev. Tom Griffith stated years ago in his article in *Open Hands*, "Give a Cheer for Our Evangelical Brothers and Sisters":

> Although the creeds of our denomination pay lip service to the idea that scripture is "authoritative" and "sufficient for faith and practice," many of us have moved far beyond that notion in our own theological thinking.

He continued,

> We are only deceiving ourselves—and lying to our evangelical brothers and sisters—when we deny the shift we have made. . . . We have moved far beyond the idea that the Bible is exclusively normative and literally authoritative for our faith. To my thinking, that is good! What is bad is that we have tried to con ourselves and others by saying, "we haven't changed our position."[4]

But for over forty years we have had a very public and divisive debate about our church's sexual ethics. Our differences regarding this important and sensitive topic have become painfully apparent. That division has grown to the point that The United Methodist Church is now in crisis. So much so that in 2016 the General Conference instructed the Council of Bishops to create a commission to develop a plan to end the rancor that has come to characterize General Conferences and much of the life of the church.

Even with our differences regarding sexuality and marriage, we have been able to stay together as a church so far because we have had a common practice. We committed ourselves to welcoming all people to receive the ministries of the church, regardless of how they identified in terms of gender or sexual preference. We also agreed that our pastors would not marry same-gendered couples, nor would "self-avowed practicing homosexuals" be ordained to the ministry. Though evangelical United Methodists believe Scripture speaks clearly against same-sex practice, we could live in a church with different opinions because we had a gracious, biblical position we all covenanted to uphold.

Of course, that's where we were, not where we are. One of our US jurisdictions has now elected a married, lesbian bishop who has stated that she has presided at approximately fifty "holy union" ceremonies for gay couples.[5] Many other pastors (including at least one bishop) have performed same-sex marriages, and the defiance of some has been met with as little as a twenty-four or forty-eight hour suspension. Others have been tasked with writing a paper on why the church should liberalize its teachings on marriage. In other instances, bishops have completely dismissed complaints filed against pastors who performed same-sex weddings.

At this point, a number of annual conferences and boards of ordained ministry have defiantly and publicly rejected our church's ordination standards. And even though our Judicial Council has ruled their defiance out of order, at least two have voted to ignore the council's decision. One bishop, in defiance of the church, has even commissioned and ordained openly gay, partnered clergy.

In a recent address, Bishop Scott Jones stated, "Twelve of our [US] annual conferences are in schism right now. They are unwilling to live by our covenant and that places them in schism. This is the first time that bishops and conferences have deliberately disobeyed the General Conference since 1844."[6]

Twelve annual conferences. That's over one-fifth, and there are others who do not live by the *Discipline*; they just haven't stated so publicly.

He could have added that an entire jurisdiction is now in schism. When the Western Jurisdiction elected and the Western College of Bishops consecrated Karen Oliveto to the episcopacy, they purposefully separated themselves from the teachings of the church and the covenant that unites us.

Before we can begin to answer the question, "Are we better together?," we must first ask, "Are we together?" Then we need to answer that question honestly. We believe, regrettably, that the only honest answer to that question is to frankly acknowledge we are not.

Many of our churches no longer use official United Methodist curriculum in their classes because they do not trust it. Many of our congregations no longer pay all of their apportionments because several of our boards and agencies are unaccountable to the local church and promote progressive causes contrary to Scripture. Many of our largest churches no longer include "United Methodist" in their names because they believe our "brand" has been tainted and therefore being associated with it harms their ministry. Some churches, including two of our largest, have even left the denomination because they felt the turmoil in the church impeded their ministry. Many pastors roll their eyes when the Council of Bishops speaks about unity; they know the council is no more united than the rest of the church. For nearly fifty years it has failed to lead in a way that fosters unity or creates a growing church.

Are we still one church? If we are, then we cannot act as if we are two. If we are two churches, then we should no longer pretend to be one.

I (Rob) was recently on a panel with a high-level United Methodist Church official regarding sexuality and the future of the church. She stated that in families there are often different opinions. If we talk about our differences, she said, it can make Thanksgiving dinner or the Christmas holidays difficult, but we stay together because we are family. We don't allow our different opinions to divide us. She ended her remarks by encouraging all United Methodists to "stay at the table."

I responded that her analogy was a very good description of where we had been. But it did not describe where we are now.

I stated that we are no longer a family with different opinions. We are a marriage in which one partner is unwilling to live by the covenant that holds us together. I asked her, "What should my wife do if she discovered I was being unfaithful to our marriage covenant and I told her that I was going to continue to be unfaithful?" I asked the audience, "If I told my wife that I felt justified in my actions and that it was wrong for her to think about leaving—that she should stay at the table and let me continue to cheat on her, what should she do?" I asked the group, "How should my wife respond if I told her that it was closed-minded and unchristian of her to leave because we are better together? Our finances are better together, we're raising a family together, and it would be too disruptive for us to separate. For all of those reasons, should she stay with someone who was unfaithful to her?" Finally, I said, "If my wife agreed to let me cheat on her and she refused to stand up for herself or the vows we took or the health of our family, would you respect my wife? Would you think her admirable and Christlike, or would you think her weak and lacking of self-respect?"

Every pastor who has been ordained in the United Methodist Church and every layperson who has joined since 1972 knew or should have known the church's position that the practice of homosexuality is incompatible with Christian teaching. Over thirty years ago (1984), General Conference voted to prohibit the ordination of "self-avowed practicing homosexuals." And for more than twenty years (beginning in 1996) the church has instructed pastors not to perform same-sex marriages. Of course, persons who disagree with the church's positions have every right to advocate for change. But what they do not have is the right to defy our teachings and at the same time condemn and attempt to shame others who support the church's views.

We in the United States must constantly remind ourselves we are a global church. Therefore, we must recognize that the vast majority of United Methodists believe our teachings are graciously stated and well grounded in Scripture and rooted in two thousand years of Christian tradition. They have been taught and practiced by Christians in all times and in all places, and still are today. Only a small and struggling minority of US Protestant churches has endorsed teachings to the contrary. We should not strive to be like them.

In the course of this book, we will argue that our positions regarding the Scriptures, sexuality, and a way forward are correct. However, we readily acknowledge there is little likelihood we will persuade people to think or believe differently than they already do. After forty-five years of debate, most United Methodists have settled opinions regarding the most contentious issues before us. And frankly, we have no interest in creating a scenario where one side gains enough adherents to declare itself the clear winner and the other side the loser. People on all sides are sincere in their beliefs and committed to them. For the sake of justice, progressives feel duty bound, on their reading of Scripture, to work for the full inclusion of LGBTQ+ persons in every aspect of the church. We evangelicals cannot change our position without, in our own minds, compromising our belief in the inspiration and the authority of the Bible. That's something we will never do.

What's the solution? More fighting and endless debate? Stricter rules and stronger punishment? Another forty years of delusional thinking that if we just stay at the table, debating and arguing with one another, we will be able to reconcile irreconcilable positions? No. Now is the time for us to honestly acknowledge we are no longer together, and pretending we are is not a viable option. The best way forward is a fair and amicable separation, where both sides are free to pursue what they believe God is calling them to do.

2

DIVIDED ON BIBLICAL INTERPRETATION AND THE AUTHORITY OF SCRIPTURE

During a thirty-minute sermon on the broad topic of the scriptural authority, a pastor spent two minutes carefully but clearly defending The United Methodist Church's sexual ethics and its teachings on marriage. The sermon was delivered in July 2017.

In an open letter to the pastor, a former member who identifies as a lesbian responded: "Your theology *literally* kills people . . . you wantonly condemned queer people because you felt safe in the authority of a pulpit . . . your opinion is actively working to kill me and my siblings in Christ."[1]

This response, which unfortunately is not unique, is indicative of how divided some United Methodists are over the authority of Scripture, the interpretation of the Bible, and the debate over the church's sexual ethics, including its teachings on marriage and its ordination standards. The debate, played out over forty-six years and at twelve General Conferences, has only succeeded in clarifying the wide gap between those who support and those who oppose the church's teachings. Nearly fifty years of dialogue, conversation, and roundtable discussions have failed to narrow the differences.

Two of the most important matters at the root of the debate are the tightly intertwined subjects of biblical interpretation and the church's understanding of scriptural authority. It is now abundantly clear that United Methodists of good faith and conscience interpret and weigh very differently certain passages pertaining to the church's sexual ethics and its teachings on marriage. Even more fundamentally, they have different understandings of how scriptural authority should be deployed when it comes to discerning God's will for the church. In short, as they should, biblical interpretation and scriptural authority loom large when it comes to the church's theological confessions and its ethical teachings.

In this chapter, we want to review the profound differences United Methodists have regarding biblical interpretation and the role of scriptural authority. Having done so, we will then consider whether people holding these views are really better together.

The United Methodist Church and Scriptural Authority

John Wesley's High View of Scripture

John Wesley, like many eighteenth-century Church of England clergy, had a very high view of Scripture. He understood how the early church was profoundly shaped by it and how it in turn shaped the Christian canon of Scripture. Wesley, like many of his contemporaries, believed the Holy Spirit was powerfully at work in every aspect of the formation of the Bible. For him, the people who wrote Scripture, the scribes who faithfully copied and transmitted it, and the great church councils that canonized it were all divinely inspired and directed by the power of the Holy Spirit.[2]

Furthermore, Wesley fully ascribed to the Church of England's sixth Article of Religion entitled "On the Sufficiency of the Holy Scriptures for Salvation." When, in 1784, he amended the articles for the Methodist Episcopal Church in America, he saw no reason to modify its statement. He truly believed, "HOLY Scripture containeth all things necessary to salvation," and that it included "those Canonical Books of the Old and New Testament, of whose authority was never any doubt in the Church."[3]

Wesley also subscribed to the Church of England's twentieth Article regarding its power "to decree Rites or Ceremonies, and authority in Controversies of Faith." Even more so, he would have fully endorsed the check on the church's power in the Article's remaining portion:

> And yet it is not lawful for the Church to ordain any thing that is contrary to God's Word written, neither may it so expound one place of Scripture, that it be repugnant to another. Wherefore, although the Church be a witness and a keeper of Holy Writ, yet, as it ought not to decree any thing against the same, so besides the same ought it not to enforce any thing to be believed for necessity of Salvation.[4]

In short, Wesley warmly affirmed the English Reformation's high view of Scripture. Its writing, transmission, and canonization were all done under the guidance of the Holy Spirit, and it was authoritative for the church and its people.

However, Wesley's high view of Scripture should not be mistaken for a naive fundamentalism. His many sermons and writings give evidence to his thorough familiarity with the Bible, and to its richness and complexity. As David Watson has written, "[He] was a man immersed in the Bible."[5] He was also deeply conversant with the treasure house of biblical interpretation stretching back from his own time, through the Reformation, the Middle Ages, and to the early church fathers. As a well-educated, infinitely curious, and astutely observant man, Wesley was also acquainted with the works of Enlightenment philosophers like John Locke, René Descartes, and David Hume. In short, while he professed to be a "man of one book," he was familiar with many.

Consequently, through his own reading of Scripture, the interpretations of others, philosophical works in general, and his own keen observations of the world and the people around him, Wesley readily acknowledged that the meaning of the Bible is not always readily apparent. So in his Preface to *Sermons on Several Occasions*, he explains his approach to reading it:

> Is there a doubt concerning the meaning of what I read? Does anything appear dark or intricate? I lift up my heart to the Father of lights: "Lord, is it not thy Word, 'If any man lack wisdom, let him ask of God'? Thou 'givest liberally and upbraidest not'. Thou hast said, 'If any be willing to do thy will, he shall know.' I am willing to do, let me know, thy will." I then search after and consider parallel passages of Scripture, "comparing spiritual things with spiritual". I meditate thereon, with all the attention and earnestness of which my mind is capable. If any doubt still remains, I consult those who are experienced in the things of God, and then the writings whereby, being dead, they yet speak.[6]

What marks this passage is Wesley's deep sense of trust in God and God's word for us. He is confident God will guide him in his reading and interpretation. When he is perplexed, he reads the text akin to what we today refer to as a canonical approach, "search[ing] after and consider[ing] parallel passages of Scripture." And "if any doubt still remains," he turns to the wisdom and guidance of Christian ancestors, believing God will use their interpretations of text to enlighten his own understanding of it. He trusts that God will, through the presence of the Holy Spirit, illumine his understanding. And he is confident that illumination will be in conformity with the what the church has taught in all time and all places, rather than some novel or esoteric insight that would lead him and others astray.

For Wesley, the Bible was the pathway to God, the way of salvation. For that reason, it was completely worthy of his trust and the trust of others. In his preface to notes on the New Testament, Wesley writes:

> The Scripture therefore of the Old and New Testament, is a most solid and precious system of Divine truth. Every part thereof is worthy of God; and all together are one entire body, wherein is no defect, no excess. It is the fountain of heavenly wisdom, which they who are able to taste, prefer to all writings of men, however wise, or learned, or holy.[7]

There is no evidence to suggest Wesley ever deviated from his high view of Scripture.

United Methodism and the Authority and Interpretation of Scripture

For most of the first 150 years of American Methodism, Wesley's high regard for Scripture profoundly shaped the way nearly all

Methodists read the Bible. This is not to deny the influence of other interpreters, but only to acknowledge that there was no serious attempt to challenge, alter, or even substantially enhance the Wesleyan way of reading the Bible.

However, with the rise of an increasingly college-educated and seminary-trained clergy in the later 1800s and early 1900s, other ways of reading the Bible began to influence the church. At least initially, these interpretive strategies were not taught with the intention of challenging the Wesleyan way of reading and interpreting it. The aim was to equip clergy with a better sense of the historical and cultural contexts of ancient Israel and the early church and the way historical and cultural currents shaped the writing, transmitting, and ultimately the canonization of Scripture.

Increasingly among seminary-trained clergy, historical-critical methods for reading the Bible began to supplant the Wesleyan approach we have outlined above. Many pastors attempted to employ these methodologies to help broaden the laity's appreciation of the Bible's background. In faithful and skilled hands, this approach has helped illuminate the biblical world and deepen people's understanding of and connection with the faith of the ancient Israelites and early Christians. But just as often, sermons steeped in these methods sound like dry history lectures. At their worst, they cast doubt on some of the church's core doctrinal confessions like the virgin birth of Christ and the Resurrection. To this day, some United Methodist pastors continue to lean too heavily into these biblical interpretive strategies for constructing a sermon, giving little attention to the marvelous, mysterious, and wonderful ways God seeks to redeem his people through Jesus' death and resurrection.

With the creation of The United Methodist Church in 1968, prominent church theologians saw an opportunity to articulate an approach for discerning God's will that respected Wesley's high view of Scripture yet was also more contemporary and intellectually sophisticated. Albert Outler, a leading United Methodist theologian, championed the idea of the "Wesleyan Quadrilateral," that is, the utilization of Scripture, church tradition, reason, and experience to discern God's will for his people, both corporately and personally. Although Wesley never used the term *quadrilateral* himself, Outler maintained that the approach faithfully systematized what Wesley implicitly practiced.

Before long, Outler himself recognized the word *quadrilateral* was an unfortunate choice. It implied all four approaches for discerning God's will were equally valid and therefore should be equally weighted, whereas (as Outler recognized) Wesley always regarded Scripture as the primary source of authority. Furthermore, some clergy, and consequently some laity, substituted a modern understanding of the term *experience* for what Wesley had in mind. To be fair, Outler and other Wesleyan scholars understood "experience" as Wesley himself had understood it. But in the late 1960s and early 1970s, it was easy to assume "experience" was all about one's broad, personal experiences of life, rather than Wesley's conception of the vivifying experience of the Holy Spirit working in one's life as God's grace justified and sanctified a believer.

Outler and other Wesleyan theologians rectified the error, but not before serious damage was done by those who found freedom in the idea that tradition, reason, or experience could just as easily lead the way in discerning God's will as a reliance on Scripture. Such an idea runs counter to a critically important section of the *Book of Discipline* called "Our Theological Task." In that section of the *Discipline*, the categories for discerning God's will—Scripture, tradition, reason, and experience—are carefully explicated, but the term *quadrilateral* is never used, and the emphasis clearly falls on the primacy of Scripture, with the other avenues feeding into the royal road of God's word (*Book of Discipline*; ¶105).[8]

Although this approach has received learned and trenchant critical evaluations,[9] it remains the accepted means for discerning God's will among United Methodists. For all its problems, it provides a faithful framework for affirming The United Methodist Church's core doctrinal convictions about Scripture, the Triune God, creation, humankind, God's mighty acts of salvation culminating in Jesus' death and resurrection, and the vivifying power of the Holy Spirit at work in the church catholic. Furthermore, the approach simultaneously provides necessary boundaries, but still plenty of room for further theological reflection as the people of the church attempt to live faithfully in their own time and place.

Challengers

In recent years, there have been explicit and implicit attempts to significantly modify or even supplant the Wesleyan approach to Scripture. Interpretive strategies that fall more or less under the rubric of postmodernism have undoubtedly influenced some United Methodist pastors and theologians. Postmodernism is a broad and diverse movement across many disciplines, and it is difficult to characterize it too specifically. But generally speaking, it is marked by a radical questioning of institutions, beliefs, values, and literature. What we conventionally regard as stable and take for granted—things like churches, doctrines, truth, justice, and sacred texts—postmodern critics tend to regard as mere constructs. The constructed beliefs, values, and texts are marshaled for some agenda—usually to validate and perpetuate the power of the constructed institution, which invariably serves the few at the expense of the many.

But what is constructed can also be *deconstructed*. According to postmodern literary theory, authoritative texts such as the Bible should be approached with suspicion. Key questions must be asked of every book, chapter, and story, questions like: Whose interest is being served in the telling of this story? How is the particular story being told actually marginalizing and suppressing others? How does the narrative preserve the power of the elites? Who were and are the keepers of the authoritative texts?

According to some postmodern critics, the answers to these questions, when asked of the Bible, reveal a god fashioned to justify patriarchy, perpetuate monarchy, and bolster the authority of religious elites. The kingdoms of Judah and Israel, on this reading, were little more than authoritarian states where the top one to two percent regularly oppressed and intermittently forced the many to serve in their wars of aggression. One example of this may be seen in Robert and Mary Coote's book *Power, Politics, and the Making of the Bible*. They argue, "The Bible was produced out of power struggles among rich men, as many down through the ages have recognized; thus rich men were its consumers and dominate its history."[10]

Put crassly, according to a postmodern interpretation, truth, justice, and reality are whatever the powers that be construct them to be. Therefore, the task of the literary critic who reads the Bible is to deconstruct the biblical stories in order to unmask the powerful. Postmodern interpretations, therefore, often turn biblical narratives on their heads.

Hence, the story of the Exodus is not one of a gracious God leading his people to liberation and joyful obedience, but actually a story of continued enslavement. When deconstructed by a postmodern literary critic, we might be invited to read the story as one written by an aristocratic priestly class seeking to validate its intermediary role between a vengeful god and a people bent on wickedness. A gracious God does not lie behind the story, but rather a self-serving religious class intent on justifying its power.[11]

Ezra and Nehemiah, according to a postmodern reading, are little more than glorified, and possibly invented leaders of a relatively rich elite intent on reasserting their power over "the people of the land" as they return to Jerusalem. Again, according to a postmodern critique, God's grace is not driving the history, but rather a powerful few are actually constructing a story to legitimize their right to rule others.[12]

Such readings carry over into the New Testament. Paul, on a postmodern reading, is no champion of grace, but rather a power-hungry misogynist, bent on leveraging a fantastic story about a crucified and resurrected Messiah in order to deceive the gullible and poor into supporting his ambition for wealth and power.[13]

As with any theory, there is some truth in it that makes it appealing. However, postmodern literary criticism is often highly reductionistic, believing all people are animated only by a drive for power and their desire to retain it. Reading such interpretations often leaves one with the impression that there is little or no room for anything good in the human spirit and that any notion of a god of truth, love, and justice is regarded as just another prop to ensure the power of the elites.

In recent years, the application of postmodern literary theory to Scripture appears to have reached its zenith, as postmodern biblical criticism seems to be less popular today than it was in the 1990s and early 2000s. But there are still United Methodist pastors and theologians who find it useful in the debate over the church's sexual ethics, teachings on marriage, and its ordination standards.

In contrast to Wesley's "hermeneutic of trust" in Scripture, postmodern theory leads with a "hermeneutic of suspicion."[14]

Finally, there is a one more approach to Scripture that bears some consideration. It is the interpretive strategy proposed by Adam Hamilton in his book *Making Sense of the Bible*. While his proposal is not necessarily a new one, it is important to consider it given Hamilton's influence in The United Methodist Church. He is the pastor of the largest United Methodist church in the United States, a leader in the centrist movement, and many of his books are widely read. The approach Hamilton describes is not intended to replace Wesley's or anything outlined in the *Discipline* regarding the primacy of Scripture. Although he never states it explicitly, one gathers he believes his proposal merely augments the others. It is also influenced by the positivistic tendencies of historical-criticism and—surely unwittingly—it bears some resemblance to a second-century interpretive approach that was ultimately rejected by orthodox Christianity.

Hamilton's proposal is proffered as an attempt to help Christians discern God's will as they turn to the Bible for guidance on complex and controversial issues. He acknowledges that the Bible is not simply a compendium of entries that anticipate correct answers to every ethical dilemma that comes before the church. In fact, as careful readers of the Bible recognize, some of the biblical stories can shock and disturb our ethical sensibilities. That being the case, Hamilton writes:

> As we read and interpret scripture, I'd suggest that there are three broad categories—let's call them buckets—that biblical passages fit into. There are passages of scripture—I would suggest the vast majority—that *reflect the timeless will of God for human beings*, for instance, "Love your neighbor as you

love yourself." There are other passages that *reflect God's will in a particular time but not for all time*, including much of the ritual law of the Old Testament. And there are passages that *reflect the culture and historical circumstances in which they were written but never reflected God's timeless will*, like those related to slavery (emphasis original).[15]

On first blush, Hamilton's "buckets" seem like a helpful and practical way of separating the wheat from the chaff. But on closer inspection, it is clear his approach to Scripture is antithetical to Wesley's and a significant departure from what is outlined in the church's *Discipline*. It also raises at least as many questions as it answers. For example, who is the final arbiter of what passages go into which buckets? What are the criteria for determining which verses, chapters, and books go where? And what comes of those portions of the Bible tossed into buckets two and three? Hamilton evidently believes he and other modern readers are equipped with the tools to do the sorting (presumably historical-critical tools aid the reader in this endeavor), and once it is done they will be left with a pristine collection of stories, sayings, and commandments that reflect God's true will.

Hamilton takes Scripture seriously and recognizes it is difficult and disturbing at times, which we find laudable. However, were people to follow his approach, it would lead to the virtual excision of parts of the Bible. Who but historians and antiquarians would continue to regularly read Bible passages "that reflect[ed] God's will in a particular time but not for all time," let alone ones that "never reflected God's timeless will"? His buckets metaphor is an inadvertent invitation to cease reading some parts of the Bible.

Although Hamilton fails to acknowledge it, the practical effects of his approach would be similar to other approaches that have been tried before. In the mid-second century, Marcion, a wealthy ship builder and convert, became convinced Christians should reject the Jewish Scriptures as well as most of the books and letters that make up the New Testament. For him and his followers, only the Gospel of Luke and a handful of Paul's letters were the inspired and authoritative word of God (that is the God of Jesus, not what Marcion saw as the "god" of the Jews, which he regarded as a malevolent force). The early church rejected Marcionism and it eventually died out as a movement.

Centuries later, Thomas Jefferson, a true son of the Enlightenment, was so confident in his ability to identify the true sayings and deeds of Jesus that he took a penknife to the Gospels. He extracted only those sayings and deeds he was convinced Jesus truly said and did and then pasted them into a very thin volume he called *The Philosophy of Jesus*. Writing to a friend about his project, he said it was like, "extracting diamonds from a dunghill." Jefferson's regard for the writers of the Gospels was not high. He referred to them as "unlettered and ignorant men," given to "superstition" and "priestcraft" (a backhanded way of criticizing both the Gospel writers and the leaders of the Roman Catholic and Anglican Churches). Jefferson was wise enough to know the majority of his fellow Americans would not appreciate his cut and paste project, so he kept it private. In the early twentieth century a limited number of the *Philosophy* were printed and presented to newly elected US Senators. The book was not widely available until the second half of the century.[16]

And in recent history a number of New Testament scholars from leading universities and seminaries participated in the Jesus Seminar project. Together, the participants read through the four Gospels and voted on the authenticity of the recorded sayings and deeds of Jesus. They used four different colored beads to rank their confidence, or lack thereof, in the Gospels writers' ability to truly capture Jesus' actual words and deeds. Their work culminated in two principle publications: *The Five Gospels: What Did Jesus Really Say?* (1996) and *The Acts of Jesus: What Did Jesus Really Do?* (1998). Not surprisingly, the Jesus Seminar's version of Jesus' words and deeds differed markedly from that of Matthew, Mark, Luke, and John.

To be sure, Hamilton's strategy for interpreting the Bible stops well short of these extreme approaches. But he gives no indication in his book that he is aware of how his proposal, if taken too far, could lead to similar results as those advocated by Marcion, Jefferson, the Jesus Seminar, or others who have proposed expunging, cutting, or sorting out the Bible. Consequently, he fails to contend with the legitimate questions and critiques such unorthodox approaches have encountered. His "buckets" proposal inadvertently invites Christians to sit in judgment of the Bible rather than the other way around. Wesley and many interpreters before and after him have been aware of the difficult and even repugnant passages we find in the Bible, but in keeping with orthodox church teaching they have never proposed explaining away or discarding portions of the Bible. They, and many contemporary biblical scholars, would be troubled by Hamilton's confidence in our ability to sort Scripture into three buckets, two of which we can effectively discard. What Hamilton regards as a means of biblical interpretation actually subverts biblical authority.[17]

Most Christians know this is way too easy and wide open to abuse. Who among us would not, on occasion, like to toss into Hamilton's second and third buckets a particular biblical story, commandment, or saying that convicts us? The human heart, as both the Bible and experience teaches us, is inclined to self-justification in order to get what it wants. At one time or another we have all watched and winced as otherwise faithful people have engaged in biblical interpretive gymnastics in order to justify their actions. And if we are honest with ourselves, we are as prone as they are to do the same.

While Hamilton's proposal is well meaning, it is antithetical to Wesleyan and orthodox approaches to Scripture. Nevertheless, some UM pastors and laity confidently regard it as a valid approach to reading and interpreting the Bible. Consequently, they often argue that our differences are not about the authority of the Scripture but only about its interpretation. That is simply not true. When some United Methodist pastors assert that some parts of the Bible never were truly God's word, that is not a statement about the interpretation of the Bible, but about its inspiration. Their view differs greatly from Wesley's statement that "Every part thereof [Scripture] is worthy of God; and all together are one entire body, wherein is no defect, no excess."[18] It is an understanding of Scripture that cannot be reconciled with the Apostle Paul's belief that "all Scripture is God-breathed and is useful for teaching, rebuking, correcting and training in righteousness" (2 Timothy 3:16). And it is contrary to the view of evangelical United Methodists who believe the whole Bible—even the parts that are difficult to understand—is God's word.

Are We Better Together?

We all struggle to understand how God inspired the Bible. None of us are fundamentalists who believe God dictated it, bypassing the knowledge, experiences, and personalities of its human authors. We do not believe God turned human beings into mindless keyboards whom he employed to bang out his word. How the process of inspiration worked is mysterious, and we all wrestle with what it means to have the word of God communicated to us in the words of human authors. Nevertheless, the United Methodist Church affirms the view of Paul and Wesley that the Scriptures are fully inspired and authoritative for us both corporately and personally. We stand with the early church and with the church universal that Scripture was inspired by God and that we must stand under its authority.

In contrast with this affirmation, over the years some United Methodist leaders have candidly admitted their approach to Scripture is a departure of the church's historical stance. In 1995, Rev. Tom Griffith wrote,

> Although the creeds of our denomination pay lip service to the idea that scripture is "authoritative" and "sufficient for faith and practice," many of us have moved far beyond that notion in our own theological thinking. We are only deceiving ourselves—and lying to our evangelical brothers and sisters—when we deny the shift we have made. . . . We have moved far beyond the idea that the Bible is exclusively normative and literally authoritative for our faith. To my thinking, that is good! What is bad is that we have tried to con ourselves and others by saying, "we haven't changed our position."[19]

And in a similar vein, well known United Methodist News Service writer Rev. Richard Peck said in 2004,

> Liberals . . . view the Bible as a library of books with different levels of inspiration and truth. A quote from Leviticus carries almost no weight with [them]. Liberals are not as quick to dismiss the letters of Paul. They well know that Paul

wrote some of the most insightful and inspirational passages in all of Scripture. At the same time, they know that he was a product of his times.[20]

The United Methodist Church's teachings on Scripture may be wrong, and liberal approaches such as these practiced within The United Methodist Church may be right. But we need to be honest and admit that on the very important issue of Scripture's authority and inspiration, we are not together. So given the very different ways United Methodists interpret the Bible and think about the authority of Scripture, Are we better together?

Those who think theological diversity is one of the greatest goods would say, "Yes, of course, we are better together! It is good to have a 'mixed-multitude' in the same church." And yes, for them this multitude ought to include even those who champion approaches to Scripture that run counter to Wesley, our *Discipline*, and classical Christian hermeneutics. In this view, diverse approaches and opinions challenge us and force us to contend with interpretations we might be unaware of or simply want to avoid because they threaten cherished beliefs. Diversity might make us uncomfortable, they reason, but in the end it enriches us and make us better followers of Jesus.

We think not. The church's mission is not to be a debating society, a faculty lounge, or a perpetual town-hall meeting. Its mission is to proclaim the gospel in word and deed. To do this effectively, there must be a modicum of shared beliefs about the Bible, how the community of faith reads it and understands it, the authority it is willing to ascribe to it, and the ethics it derives from it. A church that ranks a diversity of interpretations too highly seldom if ever becomes the idealistic vision described above. Rather, where there is too much diversity regarding the interpretation and authority of Scripture, there is factionalism and therefore disunity. Unfortunately, this is where The United Methodist Church is today and where it will be tomorrow, until we recognize a truly united church cannot long endure the push and pull between such vastly different approaches to interpreting the Bible and understandings of Scriptural authority.

3

DIVIDED ON SEXUAL ETHICS

This chapter will come as no surprise. In fact, it's the reason for this book. The United Methodist Church is deeply divided regarding whether God blesses homosexual relations. Votes at General Conference indicate the depth of our differences. Depending on whether the issue is the incompatibility of homosexual practice with Christian teaching; same-sex marriage; or ordaining self-avowed, practicing homosexuals, the church's position is usually upheld by a majority that ranges from 53 percent to 60 percent. In secular politics, these margins would be celebrated as clear victories. But in a church hoping to be a family, these numbers indicate that we are divided, many of us are hurting, and nobody is really winning.

We have witnessed this division at General Conference every four years since 1972. Not only has the debate been emotional and at times acrimonious, but several conferences have been brought to a halt as pro-LGBTQ+ demonstrators have taken over the floor and at times the agenda. In Pittsburgh in 2004, someone felt compelled to display their anger and sadness by destroying the conference Communion chalice, and in Fort Worth in 2008, demonstrators draped the Communion table in black.

Legislative attempts to breach the divide have been put before General Conference on more than one occasion. Rather than prohibiting or approving of homosexual relations, the proposed legislation would have had the church state that good people see these issues differently or simply admit that we are a divided church.[1] All such attempts have failed to gain a majority.

After the 2012 General Conference reaffirmed the church's position regarding sexual ethics, Bishop Melvin Talbert stated to a group that had gathered in the Love Your Neighbor Tabernacle: "The derogatory rules and restrictions in the *Book of Discipline* are immoral and unjust and no longer deserve our loyalty and obedience. Thus the time has come for those of us who are faithful to the Gospel of Jesus Christ to do what is required of us." With several other bishops standing near in support, he then called upon the more than 1,100 pastors who had signed a pledge to marry gay couples to do so and to "stand firm."[2]

At the most recent General Conference in Portland, 2016, I (Rob) met with ten of the best-known leaders within the denomination, representing conservatives, centrists, and progressives for several hours with a number of bishops, including the president of the Council of Bishops, Bishop Bruce Ough. We were brought together to discuss the future of the church. What was scheduled as one, two-hour conversation turned into four meetings over several days. With enough time to listen to each other and understand the depth of conviction that generated our differences, the consensus was that our differences were irreconcilable and a parting of the ways was either the best option available or simply inevitable. Before a motion was made on the conference floor to create a commission to resolve our differences regarding sexuality, this group requested that Bishop Ough take to the council our request that a commission be formed to create a plan to divide The United Methodist Church into two or three new bodies, each free to determine its own sexual ethics. Bishop Ough did so, but the council was unwilling to support the group's recommendation.

There is a narrative I have heard often that church politics are as disrespectful and as ugly as secular politics. I have not experienced that to be true, especially when it comes to the leaders of the various movements within the church. It certainly was not true of the meetings between leaders of the progressive, centrist, and conservative leaders in Portland. What characterized our time together was respect for differing views, a willingness to listen to each other, and real honesty about bedrock theological principles. It was in that environment that we came to the point of believing that what was best for the denomination was a separation where no one had to compromise their deeply held beliefs and we could all be free to pursue what we believe to be God's will for his people.

We are irreconcilably divided over sexual ethics. We can love and respect each other and still come to that conclusion.

We traditionalists affirm The United Methodist Church's position regarding sexuality. Why? Because it is biblical, balanced, and compassionate. It beautifully joins together grace and truth, and we desire neither to liberalize the United Methodist position, nor to make it more restrictive.

Our beliefs regarding marriage and same-gender sexual relations agree with nearly two thousand years of Christian teaching. Our views are the same as those presently held by the vast majority of Christians around the world. Others may refer to themselves as "centrists" in The UMC's sexuality debate, but those of us who support the current teaching are at the center of the church's position both historically and globally. Others may feel they have received a special revelation of the Spirit that we unenlightened believers have not. Or they may believe they possess advanced abilities in interpreting the Scriptures that the church has lacked for two millennia. But we make no such claim for ourselves. We humbly and gladly stand with the church—historic, global, and United Methodist.

By stating we affirm the present United Methodist position, we mean that upholding the truth that "all persons are individuals of sacred worth" is every bit as important—if not more so—to us personally and to our theology as affirming the part of the *Book of Discipline* that states that the church "does not condone the practice of homosexuality and considers this practice incompatible with Christian teaching" (*Book of Discipline*; ¶161.G). As pastors and in doing theology, we teach our people that our first obligation is to accept and love everyone. Before we talk about the Bible's view of homosexual relations, we always state, "If you cannot love someone because of his or her sexual practices, you have a bigger problem before God than the person you cannot love."

No one should ever be threatened, demeaned, or made to feel unloved by God or unwanted by the church because of their sexual orientation. The "truest truth" about every person is not how he or she identifies in terms of gender, what they have done in the past, or whom they love in the present. What is most true about every one of us is that we are deeply loved and wanted by a gracious God who found us worthy of the death of his Son, Jesus.

For that reason, we want to be very clear that the United Methodist position we support is about sexual activity, not sexual desire. You will never find us condemning anyone because he or she is attracted to persons of the same gender. One reason we can affirm the United Methodist position is because it does not condemn or shame persons for their feelings or their attractions, but rather calls us to control our actions.

I think it might surprise people to know that the church where I (Rob) serve as pastor of discipleship has had on staff a pastor who was open about his same-gender attraction. He was a powerful preacher, an incredibly loving presence, and a champion for being in ministry with the poor. We loved him and we still do. He was committed to celibacy because of his faith, and we saw no reason that his same-gender attraction should disqualify him from ordained ministry or from serving as a leader in our congregation. We were happy for his many contributions to the life of our church, and we were sad when he left us to do campus ministry.

Also, before teaching on homosexuality, we always stress that heterosexual sin has done, and is doing, much greater harm to the church, to families and to the cause of Christ than homosexuality will ever do. Sins like adultery, promiscuity, and pornography are deeply damaging, more so than our culture and even our church often acknowledges. More people will be left out of the kingdom of God, more families will be torn apart, and the witness of the church will be more damaged because of heterosexual sin than homosexual sin.

Finally, before teaching our United Methodist doctrine that "the practice of homosexuality is incompatible with Christian teaching," we are sure to stress that same-gender sexual behavior is not a special category of sin. You will find it condemned in the

New Testament, but it is condemned alongside other sins that do not usually carry the same stigma—greed and slander, for example. Homosexual acts are not any more effective in making us guilty before God than pride, gossip, lying, or gluttony.

Why This Sin?

Then "why this sin?" That's a question we are asked frequently by those who want the church to change its position regarding homosexual practice. And it's very fair to ask it. Why must we speak out about this sin when other sins are more prevalent and destructive in the life of the church? Why must it be addressed in ways that others are not? There are three important reasons.

(1) This is the only sin the church is being asked to accept, affirm, and celebrate. A primary reason we feel compelled to talk about the practice of homosexuality in our churches (though we don't talk about it often) and write about it in our publications is that large numbers of people are trying to change the church's view. Of course, it's true that more people are guilty of greed than engage in homosexual activity. And there's no question that the New Testament condemns greed much more frequently than it does homosexuality. But no one is asking the church to declare that greed is good, that it is a gift from God, and that we should change what the church has taught about it for the past two thousand years. No one is encouraging persons with a greedy nature to fulfill their desire for more and more stuff.

A common objection, and it's a good one, is that we should speak or write just as often about divorce as we do about homosexuality. The reason we don't is because no one is asking the church to teach that divorce is a wonderful blessing that should be celebrated. No one is saying, "I know the Bible says divorce is wrong, but I think the Bible is mistaken. In fact, I'm going to get married and divorced over and over because I can and because it's my nature." People think of divorce as a most regrettable act, and they hope never to experience it. And if they do, they pray never to go through it again. Pastors offer grace to persons who go through divorce because that's the heart of God. But we also teach premarital courses in hopes of lowering the chances that marriages end in divorce.

Why this sin? Because it's the only sin the church is being asked to call good when the Bible says it's not.

(2) The authority of the Bible is at stake. We believe the Bible's message is clear and consistent in stating that same-gender sexual practice is contrary to God's will. The only way we could ever agree that homosexual activity is acceptable to God would be for us to decide that the Bible is wrong and its teachings cannot be trusted. Once we decide we are free to dismiss the Scriptures because "we know better," we deny the Bible's inspiration and its authority. Instead of standing under the Bible and its authority, we would be putting ourselves over the Bible and claiming to be more inspired than its authors. And should we ever let the culture change what we believe about the Scriptures, we would have "cultureanity," not Christianity.

Of course, the Scriptures can be difficult to interpret. Good people can read them in different ways. But when we believe the Bible's message is clear and consistent, we cannot deny its teachings without denying its authority, which is something we will never do.

(3) The healing ministry of the church is at stake. All of us are broken emotionally and sexually. Homosexuality is one form of sexual brokenness. Very often abuse, seduction at an early age, gender disturbance, and dysfunctional family dynamics play a part in a person's coming to identify as gay. When that's the case, the most unkind, unloving thing we can do is to tell a person that his or her brokenness is a gift from God and not offer the hope of emotional and sexual wholeness.

The church is called to be a healing community. If we fail to offer healing because our culture and progressive Christians want us to call brokenness "wholeness," we fail God and we fail persons who are gay.

We know men and women who have been healed of this brokenness through the love and understanding of God's people and through the power of his Spirit. We have been moved by the gratitude they have expressed for the freedom they have found in Christ. If there are others who want to experience sexual healing, we cannot let the political correctness of our culture stop the church from offering the gracious healing of God.

Why Support the United Methodist Position?

Why do we affirm the current United Methodist position regarding marriage and sexual practice? Because it reflects what the Bible teaches.

The Scriptures give us God's mind regarding sex, and they paint a beautiful picture. Sex is God's idea, his good gift to his people. We were created as sexual beings, male and female, and God's first command to humankind was to "be fruitful and increase in number" (Genesis 1:22). Obviously, sexual relations were given to us for the purpose of reproduction. But there's more to sex than that. Sex was created to bring about a genuine, "one flesh" unity (Genesis 2:24) between a couple—a real, deep intimacy (what is often described by the Hebrew word for *knowing* our partner). It's interesting that after stating that Adam and Eve were created to experience a one-flesh intimacy, Genesis tells us that they were "both naked, and they felt no shame" (Genesis 2:25). Before sin entered the picture, the giving of ourselves to our spouse sexually functioned to create a relationship of acceptance and love that allowed for complete vulnerability with no reason to hide, cover up, or protect ourselves. Sex was given to us by God for another reason—our enjoyment. One entire book of the Bible, the Song of Songs, is a celebration of the romantic and physical pleasures of sexual relations. Reproduction, emotional intimacy, and physical pleasure, any of these would make sex a great blessing. Together they make sexual relations one of God's most marvelous gifts to his children.

The sexual ethic of the Scriptures has both a positive and a negative component. Positively, marriage, as our United Methodist position states, is the spiritual, emotional, and physical union of one man and one woman. It is with this union that God began the human race. God very well might have created another arrangement. To borrow the imagery of Genesis, Adam had more than one rib. God could have created the man and then any number of women to join him in Eden. But God created one man and one woman—God obviously meant marriage to be a real partnership of equals. And there is no reason that what was created out of Adam had to be different in gender. In fact, if anything, it's unexpected and surprising that what comes from Adam is not another man, but a woman. One would expect "like to beget like." So, God's decision to create a woman to join the man, and only one woman, was purposeful and intentional. The pattern we see in the creation of humankind tells us something very important about God's will regarding how we are (and are not) to share our sexuality with other human beings.

Jesus reaffirmed the one man-one woman pattern of marriage we see in the beginning of Genesis. " 'Haven't you read,' he replied, 'that at the beginning the Creator "made them male and female," and said, "For this reason a man will leave his father and mother and be united to his wife, and the two will become one flesh"? So they are no longer two, but one flesh' " (Matthew 19:4-6). And when Paul instructs Timothy to appoint leaders in the church, one of the qualifications is that he be "the husband of one wife," (NKJV) literally "a one-woman man" (1 Timothy 3:2).

The Bible teaches clearly that God's will for marriage is one man and one woman. It's what God created in the beginning. It was reaffirmed by Jesus. And it was taught as the rule of life for faithful Christians by the early church.

In the Old Testament we often find men, even men called and anointed by God such as Abraham and David, who lived outside of God's will for marriage, engaging in adultery and polygamy. But their failure to be true to God's design for marriage is descriptive of our sinfulness, not prescriptive of God's will for our lives.

The purposeful pattern of creation, its reaffirmation by Jesus, and the church's standards for elders are all in agreement. God's good gift of sex is to be enjoyed within monogamous, heterosexual marriage.

Negatively, the Bible is clear and consistent. Sex outside of marriage, including same-gender relations, is contrary to God's will for us. The Ten Commandments, Jesus' condemnation of adultery—and lust for that matter—and Paul's prohibition against sexual immorality (*porneia*) in general, including fornication, all tell us that God limits faithful sexual activity to heterosexual marriage.

The Scriptures do not mention homosexuality often. I think we can be grateful that we do not pick up the book we read to learn about God to find that on every other page there are various sexual practices described in detail, either being condemned or commended. Depending on how you interpret them, there are no more than nine passages that deal with homosexual behavior. Some that unquestionably do are the following.

- **Leviticus 18:22:** "Do not have sexual relations with a man as one does with a woman; that is detestable."
- **Leviticus 20:13:** "If a man has sexual relations with a man as one does with a woman, both of them have done what is detestable."
- **Romans 1:26-27:** "Because of this, God gave them over to shameful lusts. Even their women exchanged natural relations for unnatural ones. In the same way the men also abandoned natural relations with women and were inflamed with lust for one another. Men committed shameful acts with other men, and received in themselves the due penalty for their perversion."
- **1 Corinthians 6.9-11:** "Do you not know that wrongdoers will not inherit the kingdom of God? Do not be deceived: Neither the sexually immoral nor idolaters nor adulterers nor men who have sex with men nor thieves nor the greedy nor drunkards nor slanderers nor swindlers will inherit the kingdom of God. And that is what some of you were. But you were washed, you were sanctified, you were justified in the name of the Lord Jesus Christ and by the Spirit of our God."
- **1 Timothy 1:9-11:** "We also know that the law is made not for the righteous but for lawbreakers and rebels, the

ungodly and sinful, the unholy and irreligious, for those
who kill their fathers or mothers, for murderers, for the
sexually immoral, for those practicing homosexuality, for
slave traders and liars and perjurers—and for whatever
else is contrary to the sound doctrine that conforms to the
gospel concerning the glory of the blessed God. . . ."

Homosexual practice is not mentioned often in the Bible, but
the message is consistent. In no passage is there a single word that
promotes, condones, or even accepts homosexual practice. Unlike
with divorce, there are no exceptions, no situations under which
it may be seen as a regrettable but understandable and acceptable
alternative. In every instance, homosexual acts are said to be
contrary to God's will for us, and therefore sinful.

It's important to note that these references to homosexual
practice are not culturally bound. They are found in both the Old
and the New Testaments. They were written for both a Hebraic
and a Greco-Roman culture.

We do not have space to consider the passages quoted above
in detail, nor is that the purpose of this book. But such work has
been done by no less a scholar than Richard B. Hays, past dean of
Duke Divinity School and George Washington Ivey Professor of
New Testament. After a careful examination of the texts referring
to homosexual practice, Hays wrote in his monumental work
The Moral Vision of the New Testament that though only a few
passages address homosexual relations, "all that do mention it
express unqualified disapproval. . . . In this respect, the issue of
homosexuality differs significantly from matters such as slavery or
the subordination of women, concerning which the Bible contains
internal tensions and counterposed witnesses. The biblical witness
against homosexual practices is univocal."[3]

Regarding same-sex relations, the Bible is clear and consistent. And for nearly fifty years, The United Methodist Church has gotten it right. All persons are persons of sacred worth, deeply loved by God. God's design for marriage involves one man and one woman, and sex outside of a monogamous heterosexual relationship, including same-gender relations, is contrary to God's will. The United Methodist Church is right to affirm both the positive and negative aspects of the Bible's sexual ethic. And we are happy to affirm the United Methodist position as our own.

What are some objections that persons with a pro-LGBTQ+ agenda make to applying what the Bible teaches to our present time? Following are the most common arguments we hear against doing so.

(1) There are many activities the Old Testament condemns that we practice today. Why do we choose to follow what it says about homosexual practice but not about other things?

The question is a good one and very interesting. It's just not germane to the topic at hand. First, an answer to the question, and then the reason why it's not pertinent to our discussion of homosexual practice.

The answer to the question is that we find in the Old Testament different kinds of laws. There are civil laws—how a society is organized, which actions it condemns, and what punishments are to be imposed when its laws are broken. Societies differ, for example, on what drugs are legal, the age at which someone can marry, what punishment is appropriate for premeditated murder. You may agree or disagree with these laws, but no one thinks that one society's civil or criminal laws should apply to another society. The Old Testament civil laws were given to Israel. They were never intended for Christians or for non-Jewish secular states.

We also find in the Old Testament many religious laws. These included what dress was appropriate for priests, what offering should be made on what days, and how one "cleansed" oneself in preparation for worship. Again, these laws were specific in their intent. They applied to the practice of the ancient Jewish religion. We Christians are grateful for our Jewish heritage, but we do not practice the Jewish faith nor did Jesus teach that we should adopt all its practices. Many do not apply to us.

But there is a third category of law in the Old Testament. These are moral laws. They tell us what is right and wrong in the sight of God, and they apply to all people at all times in all cultures. These do apply to us. Most, if not all, were reaffirmed by Jesus and the apostles. They include the Ten Commandments, loving our neighbor, and not practicing usury, for example. Moral laws do not change from culture to culture or from time to time because God's nature and character do not change.

It can be a challenge to determine which laws fall into which category. Were certain dietary restrictions (no pork or shellfish) civil laws or religious laws? Scholars debate that question. But they certainly were not moral laws. Jesus declared all foods clean. So, it's not hypocritical to say that Old Testament prohibitions against bacon and lobster don't apply to Christians.

As interesting as the question of why do we follow some Old Testament laws and not others is, it has nothing to do with our debate concerning the practice of homosexuality. That's because the New Testament is as clear as the Old in teaching that such relations do not please God. So, even should one conclude that all Old Testament laws are no longer binding on us in any way, it would not override the biblical witness against homoerotic behavior.

(2) But Jesus didn't say anything about homosexuality. If he didn't condemn homosexual relations, why should we?

Again, this is an interesting question and one we hear quite frequently. Books have been created with a title on the cover in bold letters, *Everything Jesus Said About Homosexuality*. Upon opening the book, we are expected to be surprised that the pages are blank. And the point is made, supposedly, that if we are followers of Jesus and he said nothing about homosexuality, then we have no basis for being against it. This is clever, but hardly dispositive.

The smallest amount of thinking allows us to see how fallacious this argument is. No one doubts Jesus lived in a culture that prohibited homosexual practice. No scholar has made the case for the existence of some first-century Jewish group that taught the practice was compatible with Jewish culture norms. No one has argued that Jews in the time of Jesus thought any of their Scriptures endorsed such a practice.

Given what we know about the world in which Jesus lived and his allegiance to the Scriptures he appealed to, it is a serious mistake to assume his silence on the practice is somehow an endorsement of it. Schooled in the law and prophets, he regarded heterosexuality as the norm and clearly taught that marriage is between one man and one woman. Furthermore, we can be sure that if Jesus did happen to affirm or even countenance the practice of homosexuality, we would have heard about such a radical view from either his followers or more likely his Pharisaic enemies. It is far more likely that Jesus did not specifically address the practice because it was a non-issue for the vast majority of first-century Jews living in Palestine. In short, he did not need to publicly censure a behavior no one was openly endorsing.

Jesus was willing to suffer the ire and even the persecution of the religious leaders of his day for welcoming sinners and outcasts. He had no trouble condemning traditions and beliefs that harmed people and kept them from experiencing the grace of God. Had he believed the views of his culture regarding homosexual practice were wrong-headed, he would have spoken out against them just as clearly. The argument that Jesus said nothing about homosexuality and thereby wanted his followers to infer that he was for gay relationships is simply preposterous.

What Jesus embodied, and what we must embrace, is a beautiful combination of grace and truth. Like Jesus we must genuinely and sacrificially love everyone regardless of their sin and do all we can to protect the worth and the dignity of those who are attacked for their sin. That's grace. But we must also be willing to say, "go and sin no more" as Jesus said to the woman caught in adultery (John 8:11 NKJV). That's truth. And that's Jesus.

(3) I know many gay persons who love Jesus, who are faithful church members, and who are committed to prayer and serving others. If you knew people like this, you would change your views and agree they are good, exemplary Christians.

I don't doubt you know many gay persons who are truly fine individuals and committed church members. Most of us do. I know many fine individuals who love Jesus, tithe, and serve others in marvelous ways. Some of them are proud. Others are greedy. Sad to say, I've known people who prayed and cared for the poor in the name of Jesus who at the same time were committing adultery. It's hard for me to admit, but thirty years ago in a small Texas town one dear eighty-year-old saint of the church I pastored dropped the N-word in my presence. Am I to decide that maybe the Bible is wrong about pride, greed, adultery, or prejudice because I've known some really wonderful Jesus-loving people who practiced such traits? Of course not. That's not how we make theological decisions or determine what pleases God. But that's what this argument would have us do regarding same-sex relations.

We can possess great compassion for people who have committed their lives to Christ and who struggle with sin—any sin. Hopefully, we can, because it includes all of us. I need that compassion and grace, and so do you. But what we cannot do is change the word of God because we or good people we admire have a difficult time being obedient to what it teaches. The most caring approach is to join together grace and truth as Jesus did—loving people like no one else but also telling the truth like no one else. Misrepresenting God's Word to people does them no favor. In fact, it may do them great harm.

(4) The Bible doesn't really speak to loving gay relationships. Paul didn't know about homosexuality the way we do today, so he was condemning temple prostitution and pederasty—not committed relationships between equals.

Our response to this objection is simply to ask, How do you know this? How can you say for sure what Paul was and was not familiar with? We are told that there have always been gay persons. I would assume that even in ancient times there were gay persons who wanted loving, committed relationships. Though Jewish culture would have condemned such relationships, some contemporary cultures did not.

Paul traveled extensively throughout the northeastern quadrant of the Roman Empire. He was immersed in Greco-Roman culture. He was "the apostle to the Gentiles." He lived in their world, spoke their language, quoted their poets, understood their philosophy, and debated their scholars. There is little or no support for the idea that he was unaware of the variety of sexual relationships that were practiced in the ancient world. Rather, his supposed naivety about those relationships is little more than a modern, patronizing presumption intended to delegitimize his views. There is no evidence to support such an argument.

Ben Witherington is the Amos Professor of New Testament for Doctoral Studies at Asbury Theological Seminary and member of the doctoral faculty of University of St Andrews in Scotland. His biblical knowledge has been featured on the History Channel, the Discovery Channel, NBC, CBS, ABC, and CNN. In a remarkable paper titled "Gender Matters: Human Sexuality and the Bible Yet Again," Dr. Witherington reviews the writings of ancient authors, Jewish and Gentile, regarding homosexuality. He concludes: "Another fallacy which should be mentioned at this juncture is the notion that modern same-sex experiences between consenting adults have no analogies in the Biblical world, and that therefore the Bible has nothing to say about such experiences. This is clearly *historically false*, and of course is just a way of trying to hold at arm's length what the Bible does say about same-sex sexual practices."[4]

Witherington recognizes that same-sex relations between consenting adults did occur in Paul's time. So there is little reason to think Paul's prohibition of same-gender relations is aimed only at temple prostitution or pederasty. In the passage where he addresses same-sex practice in the most detail, he first states "even their women exchanged natural sexual relations for unnatural ones" (Romans 1:26). Obviously, this has nothing to do with temple prostitution or pederasty, which is an older, more powerful male using a younger male for his sexual pleasure. In the next verse he describes men who "*in the same way* . . . also abandoned natural relations with women and were inflamed with lust for one another" (emphasis added). Again, the context undermines the idea that Paul is necessarily referring to prostitution or pederasty. The desire itself is contrary to the natural state God willed for human beings and the sin is acting on those desires.[5]

(5) Where is the sin if the relationship is consensual? This line of reasoning is particularly sad and disturbing because it is usually stated by clergy. Often a pastor raising this objection will refer to some noted theologian and make a case from his or her writings that all sin is "sin against the community." Consequently, they argue, if no one is injured or harmed, how can sex within a loving, same-gendered relationship be sinful?

What is so distressing about this argument is its anthropocentric (human-centered) understanding of sin. In classical theology sin is an offense because it is rebellion against God. It is theocentric (God-centered). But when we say there is no sin unless another human being or the community is harmed, we now put human beings in the place of God. Why is something sinful? Not because it displeases God or because it rebels against ultimate goodness, but only because someone else is offended or harmed. This is the classic human failing—we put ourselves in the place of God.

A man is alone on a deserted island. Can he not be guilty of pride, the greatest of all sins, simply because there is no one else on the island that his pride can harm? Did Eve not sin by eating the fruit until she gave Adam a piece to consume? And what was Adam's sin? He only did what Eve desired. They were mutually supportive in eating from the forbidden tree. They were good with each other's choice. They certainly suffered the consequences of their sin, but first and foremost, it was God who was offended by their sin.

The ultimate sin in the garden was not desiring the taste or the beauty of the fruit, but acting on the serpent's lie that eating the fruit would make them like God. They desired to and tried to take his place and determine right and wrong independent of God. This is exactly what an anthropocentric definition of sin does. The community, not God, decides what is good and what is evil. (And, of course, this begs the question of who decides what the community believes is good and who determines if the community has actually been harmed.)

We must decide. Will we be classical Christians with a theocentric understanding of sin—something is wrong if it violates God's will? Or will we be people with an anthropocentric understanding of sin, believing any action or practice is legitimate as long as it is consensual or does not infringe upon the rights of another person. This argument is culturally accommodative and presumably makes Christianity more appealing to others, but it does so at the cost of one of our cardinal doctrines as historic, orthodox Christians.

(6) Science has proved that people are born gay. Why would God make people that way and then tell them not to be who they are?

This statement is made so often and with such certainty that you may have come to believe it's true. But the next time you hear this, ask the person making the claim to point you to the peer-reviewed scientific studies that substantiate such a sweeping and definitive statement. You will not receive an answer.

One candidate for bishop who was being interviewed by our Texas Annual Conference delegation to General and Jurisdictional Conferences, made just that claim. I asked her what research she had seen that verified her claim. She said she couldn't quote a specific study right then, but there were many. I asked her to please send me the information. That was sixteen years ago. I'm still waiting.

Listen, this claim is too important to simply repeat what you have heard others say because it would seem to justify your beliefs. LGBTQ+ advocates tell us all the time to be careful with our language because what we say can harm real people. I get that, and I try to be as respectful as possible, always remembering that what we are discussing is not just about an "issue;" it's about real people. But because this does involve real people—not just their happiness during this lifetime but possibly their eternity—persons in favor of gay relations and marriage need to be just as careful. Do not state as fact what you do not know to be true.

Human behavior is much too complicated to be determined by a gene or even many genes. Sexual identity and preference are not like eye color; they are created by an extremely complex interaction of biological and environmental factors. *New Scientist* reports that even Dr. Alan Sanders, whose recent study of homosexual brothers has been celebrated as proving a genetic link to homosexual orientation, cautions that "complex traits such as sexual orientation depend on multiple factors, both environmental and genetic. Even if he has hit on individual genes, they will likely only have at most a small effect on their own, as has also been seen in studies of the genetic basis for intelligence, for example."[6]

Do I believe that being gay is a choice? Not for the vast majority of people who identify as gay. I did not choose to be heterosexual, and most homosexuals do not choose to be homosexual.

But that doesn't mean that our "orientation" was predetermined at birth.

Mother Jones is a progressive magazine that produced a wonderfully balanced, lengthy article titled: "Gay by Choice? The Science of Sexual Identity." The article discusses the work of several psychologists, including feminist professor Lisa Diamond.

Dr. Diamond was awarded the Outstanding Achievement Award by the American Psychological Association Committee on Lesbian, Gay, Bisexual, and Transgender Concerns in 2011. Her work has discovered that sexual identity is much more fluid than people imagine.

The author of the *Mother Jones* article, professor of psychology Gary Greenberg, writes, "Lisa Diamond may have the best reason of all for activists to shy away from arguing that homosexuality is inborn and immutable: It's not exactly true. She doesn't dispute the findings that show a biological role in sexual orientation, but she thinks far too much is made of them. 'The notion that if something is biological, it is fixed—no biologist on the planet would make that sort of assumption.'"[7] No biologist on the planet would, but many people who know nothing about biology do. They have never read a scientific study on the causes of homosexuality, but they have no qualms stating "science has proved that people are born gay." Reading about the research, including the studies that have been used to "prove" that persons are born gay—such as what's referred to as the twin studies, the study of the hypothalamus in gays and straights, and the study of the Xq28 section of the chromosome—proves fascinating. At most, these studies point to a genetic influence, but not a hard and fast determination about one's sexual orientation. The truth is, much is unknown about how sexual orientation is determined.

Dr. Greenberg concludes, "While scientists have found intriguing biological differences between gay and straight people, the evidence so far stops well short of proving we are born with a sexual orientation that we will have for life. Even more important, some research shows that sexual orientation is more fluid than we have come to think, that people, especially women, can and do move across customary sexual orientation boundaries, that there are ex-straights as well as ex-gays."[8]

No less a scientist than geneticist Francis Collins, past head of the Human Genome Project and director of the National Institutes of Health, concluded about homosexual identity "that whatever genes are involved represent predispositions, not predeterminations."[9]

Is a person's being gay already determined at birth? No research proves that it is. In fact, responsible biologists say almost no human behavior is determined at the time of birth. The most that can be said at this point is that there may be some biological "predisposition" towards same-sex attraction but there is no predetermination—no immutable hardwiring.

If a person's sexual attractions and identity are not hardwired and most of us do not choose our desires, how do people become homosexual or, for that matter, heterosexual? I hesitate to state what I have been told by others about their experiences because (1) it's anecdotal in nature and (2) it will be offensive to some. But men who either identify as homosexual or who struggle with same-sex attraction have told me they know how they came to have the feelings they possess. For some it was being seduced by an older man who showed them real concern and affection when they felt alone. One was raped by a group of boys when he was ten years old. For some reason that experience was imprinted into his psyche and marked him and his desires. One was brought up as a girl. Others were rejected by their fathers, craved male affection, and doubted their own manhood. Women who identify as lesbian have told me of being abused by men, emotionally and physically. They came to look for love and tenderness in relationships in which they felt certain they would not be brutalized. For some of these women, their attraction to other women began late in life, after they had been attracted to and had sex with men for many years.

Is this how most people come to identify as gay? I have no idea. But I know the people I have spoken to believe that's how their same-gender attraction was formed. They don't believe "God made me that way." There is a progressive fundamentalism that does not allow people to have their own story. There is a homosexual orthodoxy that tells people you were born gay, that's your story, you need to own it, and that's the story "good gays" tell. But many gay persons know that's not the truth for them. And the science says they're right—contrary to the fundamentalist progressive view that tells them that their identities were biologically predetermined.

If you believe as I do that there are often hurtful influences that may lead someone to become gay, then you will understand when I say that we should be particularly compassionate toward gay persons. Again not all, but many have suffered greatly not just for being gay but even before they identified as gay. The pain and the mistreatment they suffered wounded them so deeply that they are sexually broken. Open your heart to gays and lesbians. We are all broken, just in different ways. We share a common humanity, and the last thing we can do in the name of Jesus is put ourselves above others or distance ourselves from them because their brokenness is different than ours. That's what the Pharisees did. But not Jesus. And not us.

(7) But you cannot tell gays they have sacred worth on one hand and on the other hand tell them that acting on their God-given nature is wrong. Homosexuals cannot be expected to abstain from their very nature and at the same time be sexually whole.

This last objection is a direct quote of a challenge I (Rob) received to an editorial I wrote. The underlying assumptions are that sexual wholeness (a) is essential to emotional health and (b) requires physical consummation to be realized.

We do believe that God's goal for us is wholeness, including physical, emotional, and spiritual well-being. But we do not believe that being sexually whole necessitates that a person be sexually active.

Jesus was not sexually active. Was he less than whole? What about the Apostle Paul? People who enter monasteries vow to abstain from sex, including individuals like Francis of Assisi and Mother Teresa. Are we to imagine that they are less than whole?

What about single Christians who decide to remain chaste until marriage or those who have never married for various reasons? Are they not sexually whole? What about those who remain chaste after a divorce or the death of a spouse? What about a soldier who is faithful to his or her spouse while away on duty for months or years at a time? They all continue to have a sexual nature. If they are not acting on that nature, does that make them less than whole persons?

We believe that each of these individuals is, or can be, sexually whole despite not being sexually active. We suggest that a sex life that honors God is what determines whether or not we are sexually whole, not how often, or if, we engage in sexual intercourse.

But, if we must, yes, we can ask people not to give into their "nature" in order to honor Christ. That's not because we tell people what's required to please God, but because he has told us what is required. As a matter of fact, a big portion of the Christian life is learning to overcome our natural desires and practicing those disciplines and ways of life that are good and healthy, in keeping with God's will for us.

Jesus calls us to a way of life that is difficult. He did not come into the world to make us happy but to make us holy. Holiness requires that we live differently from the world, crucify our pride, put others ahead of ourselves, sacrifice what we want to possess so we can be generous to those in need, restrain our anger, overcome lust, love our enemies, and bless those who curse us. All of which are difficult and very often go against our natures.

In fact, self-denial is at the heart of being a disciple. "Then he called the crowd to him along with his disciples and said: 'Whoever wants to be my disciple must deny themselves and take up their cross and follow me'" (Mark 8:34).

Crucifying our old nature is part of following Jesus. If the church fails to teach that we must abstain from the desires that would lead us away from God, we fail God and we fail those who want to be faithful to Christ.

We are not called to an easy life, but to a holy life. It's a life meant to be lived in a supportive community that accepts people regardless of their desires or their past. Those of us who believe we are called to holiness must create a warm and open community that is welcoming of broken people, no matter what that brokenness may be. If we expect people to be honest about their struggles and commit themselves to wholeness, we must assure them with our words and with our actions that they will not be judged or shamed, but respected and admired for wanting to be faithful. We must be prepared to walk with others as they walk toward holiness, knowing they will stumble just as we do. We must extend to them the same love and grace we know we depend upon for healing, life, and salvation.

As compassionate as I believe the United Methodist approach is, I am aware that many of our progressive friends within the church find it discriminatory and harmful. Reasons against homosexual practice, which we believe are based on biblical truth, they view as being less than Christ-like. Anything other than full approval of homosexual relations among consenting persons, they judge as less than loving. However, we believe that sometimes the most compassionate course of action is to tell someone the truth, even if it's a truth that person doesn't want to hear. My best friends are the ones who confront me with my selfishness, my pride, and my sins. It's not always pleasant when they do so, but I know it's meant for my good and born out of their love for me.

We cannot walk away from the United Methodist position regarding sexuality because we believe it is biblical, balanced, and compassionate. But we also know that getting the position right is only half the battle. Our theology can be right, but if we do not accept, welcome, support, and love our gay friends, brothers and sisters, our hearts will be wrong.

A dear friend of mine (Rob), Jim, now deceased, served on the General Board of Church and Society. I also served on the board at the same time, and it was not a pleasant experience for us as traditionalists. We found ourselves in the minority on practically every issue, with many votes going something like 45–8. For a board that champions diversity, it didn't feel very diverse when it came to differing views on important and controversial topics. Often, it felt that we were being patronized more than respected.

Jim often referenced his gay son as he affirmed his commitment to the United Methodist position regarding homosexuality. At one point, one of our more progressive bishops tore into him. In front of others, she looked at him disdainfully and said, "He has a name, doesn't he? Why don't you call him by his name? Why simply say, 'My son?'"

Jim said, "Bishop, he does have a name. It's John. There's a very specific reason I refer to him the way I do, even though he's not my son, not really. He's the son of my wife, Pat, by her first marriage. But I love him as if he were my own. I have for years. When I visit him in San Francisco, and the three men he lives with—all gay—I tell them that I love them too, because I do. And I tell them that if they're ever in trouble and if they ever need a place to stay, they can live with Pat and me. They'll be safe with us. I'm sorry if it offends you that I call John my son. But he is. And I love him."

You can have the right position and you can have a heart that's right. Both. My friend Jim did. So must we.

4

DIVIDED ON MISSION

Maybe our theology and our sexual ethics are different, but when it comes to mission, surely we're together, aren't we? We all agree that we want "to make disciples of Jesus Christ for the transformation of the world" (*Book of Discipline*; ¶120). Certainly, we do that better together. And maybe that's enough to keep us together. That's what some would argue.

The truth is we're not together even with respect to our mission of making disciples. I'd like to get real here. If you were to poll one hundred evangelical UM pastors and ask them to answer the question, Do you believe we are more effective in our mission by being connected to thoroughly progressive and liberal pastors? I can assure you that few, if any, would answer affirmatively. And if you were to ask, Do you believe you and your church would be more effective in ministry if the denomination required less of your time and finances, the unanimous response would be yes.

We are not together, not even when it comes to our mission. A large number of conservative churches, large and small, don't use United Methodist educational resources. Why? We don't trust them. Many of us pastors have been called by Sunday school teachers or small group leaders and have been asked why the United Methodist literature they're using questions the reliability of the Bible. We have had to go to groups bothered by study materials produced by our denomination and explain why it contradicts what we teach on Sunday mornings. And many, if not most, of us have decided the best solution is to stop using materials that undermine our people's faith in the Scriptures. Many of us agree that there are better resources available to us than those produced by the denomination, and that's what we recommend to our congregations. When we have such differing views on the best resources for making disciples, we're not together.

The United Methodist pastors I know well are, at best, ambivalent regarding the work of the General Board of Global Ministries. This is the board that is commissioned with spreading the gospel and making disciples around the globe. In recent years, the board seems to have become more open to traditional evangelism, but these pastors don't feel that it is nearly as evangelistic as it should be. And we all know evangelicals who in past years have applied to do mission work through GBGM who were rejected because of their theology. When many of us do not trust our denomination's mission agency, we're not together.

We feel that we pay huge sums of money to the denomination to support boards and agencies that add no value to our churches. We regularly receive phone calls and e-mails from members who complain that our national boards and denominational officials are promoting positions that are contrary to their beliefs. When the

General Board of Church and Society promotes the normalization of homosexual behavior and calls for divesting from companies that do business with Israel, they represent a minority of United Methodists—made evident in the fact that all such efforts have failed at General Conference. When many of our members learned that same board was a proud member organization of the radical Religious Coalition for Reproductive Choice, which supports any abortion at any time for any reason, they were not only angered—they didn't want their monies going to support such efforts. They couldn't understand why one of our boards would be part of a coalition whose agenda on abortion is so different from our United Methodist position. In fact, in our conversation with progressive, centrist, and conservative leaders at General Conference, one centrist leader said that he had called the GBCS and said, "Please stop making statements. Every time you do, I lose two tithers." The boards and agencies that we support are in no way directly accountable to the local church they are supposed to represent and resource. When many pastors hope that our members don't find out that these boards exist because it will create problems for our ministries, we're not together.

A 2009 survey, conducted by a major marketing firm hired by our denomination, revealed that laity and clergy do not have confidence in our bishops and other church leaders to effectively lead the denomination forward.[1] Although the survey is now eight years old, we strongly suspect what confidence there was then has only eroded further. In fact, at the 2016 General Conference, nearly 60 percent of the delegates voted to place term limits on our bishops.[2] Only the church's constitutional requirement that two-thirds of the delegates must vote to eliminate life tenure for them preserved the status quo. Many conservative leaders loathe

the Episcopal Fund since it requires their participation in funding the salaries of bishops who fail to enforce our covenant with integrity, as well as now one bishop who is married in a same-sex relationship. Some bishops promote theological positions contrary to our doctrines. And there are only a few bishops who can claim to have provided the kind of leadership that has resulted in real numerical growth and vitality—within the United States, almost none. Some laity have candidly told their pastors they are leaving the denomination because progressive bishops promote and countenance things contrary to Scripture and the teachings of our church. Several bishops have confided to us in private conversations that the Council of Bishops is as divided and as dysfunctional as the church. When much of the church does not trust our episcopal leaders, we are not together.

If we are honest with ourselves, we have to admit that when it comes to fulfilling our church's mission statement—making disciples of Jesus Christ for the transformation of the world—we are not better together. In fact, we're failing. We have lost membership every year since we became The United Methodist Church in 1968—fifty straight years of decline.[3] Furthermore, the latest data reveals average worship attendance in our US local churches is in free fall. On an average weekend in 2016, The United Methodist Church had 311,075 fewer people in worship than it did in 2012. That's an astounding 10.5 percent loss in just four years. Don House, a prominent United Methodist layperson and professional economist, described recent annual losses in average worship attendance as "catastrophic."[4] Those who argue we are "better together," have either ignored or failed to propose any serious plan to deal with the precipitous declines in average worship attendance and membership. We are not better together when we repeatedly fail to make more disciples of Jesus Christ for the transformation of the world. People who claim we are better together are not facing the harsh reality of the data that demonstrates we are actually and increasingly ineffective together.

Most of the current bishops are members of my generation. Growing up in the 1960s and '70s, we all repeated the same mantras, like "question authority" and "don't trust the establishment." But now that my generation *is* the establishment and my peers are the authorities, many of them employ the same heavy-handed, fear-based, authoritarian methods of control that we decried. To quote Pete Townsend of The Who: "Meet the new boss, same as the old boss."[5] When pastors and churches have to be threatened to pay their apportionments and when local churches wanting to flee the denomination have to be coerced to remain in it through appeals to the "trust clause," it's a strong indication that we're not really together.

A typical conversation among evangelical pastors about finances includes statements that go something like this: "How can I justify sending my members' hard-earned monies to causes they wouldn't support if they knew where their money was going?" "I'm frustrated to think what we could do with that money right here to spread the gospel." "We don't live in a top-down world anymore. The idea that we send our money off so people we don't know and people we don't trust will do our mission work for us, that day is over." "But our bishop has said any pastor whose church doesn't pay all of its apportionments will be moved, so what are you going to do?" "Right, what are we going to do?"

We are told that we need to allow different positions regarding sexuality because that will allow us to reach different kinds of people. Progressive churches will reach progressive people and conservative churches will reach conservative people. We'll be "better together." I'm sure progressives and self-styled centrists don't realize how offensive that line of reasoning is to conservatives. It is honestly painful for us to be in a denomination where so many leaders have a utilitarian concept of truth. "If it works, it's good. If it reaches people, then let's teach it as the gospel." The truth is not whatever sells. We're not hucksters trying to lure people into the faith, telling them what they want to hear. In fact, we are warned about this very thing in Paul's second letter to Timothy.

> For the time will come when people will not put
> up with sound doctrine. Instead, to suit their
> own desires, they will gather around them a great
> number of teachers to say what their itching ears
> want to hear. They will turn their ears away from
> the truth and turn aside to myths. But you, keep
> your head in all situations, endure hardship, do
> the work of an evangelist, discharge all the duties
> of your ministry.
>
> (2 Timothy 4:3-5)

We're not better together if reaching people means proclaiming a message that is palatable but false. That doesn't make us stronger. It makes us unfaithful.

Besides, it doesn't work. Our decline in membership and attendance is most precipitous where our churches are the most progressive. Telling people what they want to hear has no power to convict or to convert or to compel people to live as faithful disciples of Jesus.

In 1970, membership stood at 211,967 in what is today the California-Pacific Annual Conference. The North Georgia's

Annual Conference membership was 216,940. "Cal-Pac" is one of our most progressive annual conferences, and proudly so. The theology of the pastors in North Georgia is fairly mixed, but certainly more conservative than that of the pastors in Southern California. The membership of its churches is without a doubt much more evangelical.

The figures reported at their most recent annual conferences, in 2016, are revealing. Cal-Pac reported a total membership of 69,282. North Georgia's membership is 360,771.

A progressive conference poised to reach a progressive part of the country with a progressive message has declined by over 67 percent in fifty years. A traditional conference has grown by more than 50 percent during the same time. What makes these numbers even more startling is that no area of the country has grown more than Southern California since 1965. Los Angeles County has over ten million residents. Since 1965, its population has nearly tripled, growing by almost seven million residents. But The United Methodist Church in Southern California has decreased by 67 percent. Fulton County, Georgia, has a population of one million. The city of Atlanta has fewer than five hundred thousand residents. Yet, the church in northern Georgia—roughly the same size as the church in Cal-Pac in 1970—now has five times the membership of Southern California.

One might object that perhaps Southern California isn't receptive to the gospel, liberal or traditional. But many congregations have had great success in reaching people in this "hard to reach" part of the country. Five of the fifty largest Protestant churches in America are in Southern California. All of them are conservative.[6]

The same is true for the rest of the Western Jurisdiction. There are large, thriving evangelical churches in areas where we are told that churches must be progressive to reach people, while in only a few western cities do we have United Methodist churches of any size.

Will a progressive gospel win a progressive culture? No. Progressive people are not going to start getting up early on Sunday mornings, go to church, sing "On Christ the Solid Rock I Stand," and give 10 percent of their income to the cause of Christ just because we tell them that it's okay to marry gay people.

Are we better together when it comes to making disciples? We're not together. And we're not good at making disciples. And where we are the most liberal, we are the worst at bringing people to faith in Christ, making disciples, and growing churches. That doesn't make us better together. It makes us evangelicals who wish we could start new, traditional Wesleyan churches where people desperately need the gospel.

We are told that to reach millennials we must adopt a progressive sexual ethic. But none of the many denominations that have changed or compromised their traditional view of sexuality have experienced a growth in membership; in fact, they are hemorrhaging membership and worship attendees even faster than we United Methodists. The United Church of Christ (UCC) has decreased in membership by 43 percent since 1985[7] and based on current trends will lose another 80 percent of its members by 2045.[8] Average weekly worship attendance in The Episcopal Church (TEC) has declined by 32 percent since 2000.[9] Membership in the Presbyterian Church–USA (PCUSA) dropped by 32 percent between 2005 and 2015.[10] What these denominations share in common other than an inability to reach people—traditional or progressive—in any significant way is their having liberalized their sexual ethics.

Contrast these churches with movements effective at reaching millennials. Hillsong, Bethel, Passion, and even a hardcore Calvinist movement led by pastors like John Piper are actually seeing a revival, bringing together tens of thousands of young worshipers at their conferences. The work of Tim Keller, a winsome evangelical Calvinist, has built a megachurch in Manhattan, arguably one of our most secular urban centers. All of these churches are conservative in their theology.

One thing millennials hate and will run from is pandering to them and their tastes. They want authenticity, not a church that tells them what they want to hear. A church that compromises its position on sexuality because it will sell to millennials will be seen for what it is—a sellout. And millennials will sniff that out every time.

There are some, actually many, local United Methodist churches that are exceptional at bringing people to faith, making disciples, and empowering members for ministry and mission. But very few of these churches will tell you it's because they have been made better by being in a denomination with people who promote a progressive theology, by using United Methodist resources, or by spending their missional funds on causes they cannot affirm.

How are we better together? As was mentioned in the chapter on sexual ethics, at General Conference in Portland, 2016, I (Rob) met with progressive, centrist, and evangelical leaders in a special meeting called by the president of the Council of Bishops. After discussing some of our differences, a pastor stated, "We have to find a way to stay together because we are better together." I asked the question, "How so? I hear that all the time. How are we better together?"

Those in the room were bishops and leaders of some of our largest and most influential congregations. The answer, the only answer that was given was, "We do some great work fighting malaria in Africa. And UMCOR does some good work." That was it. And that's important. But nobody came up with another way we are better together.

Fighting malaria is important and we're proud of what The United Methodist Church has done to stop that terrible disease. Living in Houston in the aftermath of Hurricane Harvey, we are grateful for The United Methodist Committee on Relief. But honestly, is that why we're staying together? We can fight malaria and help people in need without remaining in a denomination embroiled in a never-ending battle over sexuality or being forced to compromise our deeply held theological beliefs.

Many of our evangelical, local United Methodist churches gladly join with Baptists, Episcopalians, Lutherans, Presbyterians, and other Methodist denominations to support great organizations like Zoe International, International Justice Mission, Hope International, the Heifer Project, and World Vision to fight poverty and disease. Local United Methodist churches send their own mission teams all over the world, led by their own people or by locals who share their beliefs and who understand that evangelism is part of making disciples. However, conservative evangelicals actually find we do better when we are together with people who firmly believe Jesus Christ is the way, the truth, and the life, and who feel no need to compromise the teachings of the Bible, regardless of denomination. And we find that our witness and our work are made worse when we are joined with United Methodists who do not share our passion for evangelism.

The early believers of the first century found themselves in a culture that was anything but Christian. The church's strict sexual ethic of faithfulness in marriage between one man and one woman and celibacy in singleness ran counter to the rampant sexual promiscuity of elite Greco-Roman culture. No Christian writer suggested the way to reach this culture was—in the name of contextualizing the gospel—to change what Jesus, the apostles, and their scriptures taught about human sexuality. They prized sexual ethics that respected men and women of all classes, honored the celibate, protected children, and served to create stable families and communities. No one proposed a solution that pastors be allowed to make up their own sexual ethic and preach whatever they thought would make people responsive to the gospel. The early church knew it was called to be different. It was glad to be different. Even though it brought them ridicule and persecution, they delighted in being countercultural.

One of the most amazing developments in the history of humankind was that the church outlasted the most powerful empire the world had ever seen. It was an empire where many of its elites reveled in licentiousness, worshiped power, and persecuted those who would not bow down to its gods and its ways. That empire was overcome by people who followed Jesus' teachings of humility, sacrificial living, and the love of neighbor and even enemy. The People of the Way offered a different kind of life than the one modeled by the elites of the Roman Empire. People who had everything, when they looked at Jesus followers, saw a different kind of life—a better life—and they came to embrace it as their own.

It would have been easy to think that a simple message of loving others and being holy of heart would never be enough to convert an empire that worshiped power and reveled in the desires of the flesh. Paul must have felt pressure to change his message when he contemplated the might of Rome. He could have looked at his message—a Messiah crucified in weakness and shame—and have been embarrassed that he had nothing more to proclaim.

But in writing to the Romans, he boldly declared, "For I am not ashamed of the gospel, because it is the power of God that brings salvation to everyone who believes" (Romans 1:16). What makes the gospel powerful enough to convert lost souls, bring hope to the despairing, transform human hearts, and even overcome an empire is the fact that it is true. When it is proclaimed clearly and compassionately, the gospel is powerful enough to convert the lost and bring salvation to sinners. It does not need to be changed, softened, or made more palatable for a progressive culture. The gospel has always been enough to transform hearts, and it always will be.

When progressives say that we are better together because we can do more together to make disciples and transform the world, they seem to suggest that our mission has little to do with theology. But how do we know what a disciple is and how a disciple lives without a theological understanding of the kingdom of God? How do we know what we are supposed to transform the world into except for what our theology tells us? Progressives and conservatives have very different theologies, so it's no surprise that our understanding of mission, world transformation, and disciple-making is very different.

It's possible we evangelicals are wrong and the progressive vision is right. I don't think we're mistaken, but it's possible. So, let's do this. Let's set each other free to pursue what we believe God is calling us to do and find out. God can bless whomever

God desires. God can use either group as God wishes. Perhaps, unfettered from those of us who keep them from ministering to our culture the way they believe is best, progressives will thrive in reaching others, their movement will grow, and under their leadership revival will break out across the land. Maybe God will bless what we traditional Wesleyans offer the world. Maybe that's how we're better—not together with two minds, but free to be single-minded in what we each believe God has called us to do.

5

DIVIDED ON A WAY FORWARD

This chapter is a substantially revised version of the article "Is There a Way Forward?" in the September/October 2017 issue of *Good News* (pages 8–14).

During the writing of this book, the Commission on a Way Forward was meeting behind closed doors in an attempt to fulfill two almost impossible tasks: produce a plan to definitively resolve the deep disagreement over The United Methodist Church's sexual ethics and maintain some semblance of church unity.

The idea of a commission was proposed and approved at the May 2016 General Conference in an effort to avoid chaos. The church's highest visioning body, the Connectional Table, had come to the quadrennial gathering with a plan to liberalize the church's teachings on marriage and to allow annual conferences to decide whether to ordain openly gay clergy. However, it quickly became apparent that even though the plan had significant support it would still be defeated, just as all previous attempts to change the church's teachings had been rejected at previous General Conferences.

The Council of Bishops (COB) knew another vote rebuffing efforts to liberalize the church's teachings could ignite waves of protest by allies of the LGBTQ+ movement. With justification, some observers feared the conference would spin out of control and prove to be a public relations disaster for The United Methodist Church. The Commission on the General Conference had contracted for heightened security and police presence at the Oregon Convention Center in Portland. All delegates and visitors had to pass through security checkpoints, and for the first several days of the conference the Portland Police Department maintained a pronounced presence in and around the convention center.

Given the dynamics of the situation, the General Conference delegates asked the Council of Bishops to give leadership and direction. The COB responded with a proposal to table all legislation having to do with the church's sexual ethics and teachings on marriage and in turn create a commission to study the controversy and propose a definitive plan for resolving the long debate. The proposal narrowly passed by a vote of 428 to 405. It gave the COB the authority to select the commission members and to convene an unprecedented called General Conference to consider a forthcoming report and proposed course of action.

While this maneuver averted chaos at the General Conference, it did not cool passions at the annual and jurisdictional conference levels in the United States. Within weeks of General Conference, several annual conferences voted to defy church law when it came to examining clergy candidates for commissioning and ordaining.[1]

Bishop Jane Middleton, on the recommendation of the New York Annual Conference's Board of Ordained Ministry, ordained and commissioned openly gay, partnered candidates.[2]

Matters took a turn for the worse when the five US jurisdictional conferences convened in July. Delegates at the Northeastern Jurisdictional Conference in Lancaster, Pennsylvania, passed several measures calling for ecclesial disobedience regarding the church's sexual ethics and ordination standards. And then, on July 15, 2016, in Scottsdale, Arizona, the Western Jurisdiction elected as a bishop of the whole church, Rev. Karen Oliveto, an openly lesbian pastor. It was widely known at the time of her election, consecration, and assignment to the Mountain Sky episcopal area that Oliveto had presided at dozens of same-sex marriages and was herself married to Robin Ridenour, a United Methodist deaconess. The votes for defiance of church law and then Oliveto's election jolted the denomination.

Initially, many United Methodists, bishops included, believed these developments had plunged the church into a crisis and warranted convening the bishops' planned commission as quickly as possible. However, it took the COB five months just to select the names of the thirty-two commission members and its three episcopal moderators. Consequently, original plans for addressing the crisis in the church as soon as 2018 were pushed back, and the Council of Bishops eventually called a special session of the General Conference for February 23–26, 2019, in St. Louis.

In the meantime the church has continued to confront growing challenges. Acts of ecclesial defiance have continued.[3] Two large and growing conservative churches in Mississippi have left the denomination with all their property and assets, and other local churches are exploring their options.[4] Several annual conferences are experiencing severe financial strains, with one characterizing its situation as a "crisis."[5] Average worship attendance continues to drop precipitously.[6] Some rank-and-file United Methodists have curtailed their giving or requested that no portion of their tithes and gifts be forwarded to the annual conference or general church. And some local churches have decided to withhold their apportionments entirely.

By the time this book is published, the Commission on a Way Forward is to have completed its work and passed along a proposed plan or plans to the COB for its consideration. The church has set aside approximately $1.5 million for the commission, and is slated to spend another $3–4 million for the called 2019 General Conference. It is no exaggeration to say the fate of the denomination hinges on the plan the commission submits to the COB and in turn what the COB presents to the delegates in St. Louis.

What follows is first a portrayal of the groups involved in the debate and then descriptions and critiques of the likely plans the 2019 General Conference delegates will consider. What is readily apparent is that The United Methodist Church is divided about a way forward and that there are no easy solutions that will satisfy everyone. The various plans, with their advocates and opponents, highlight the divided nature of the church every bit as much as our positions about Scripture, sexual ethics, and mission.

Reconcilers, Liberalizers, Conservatives

One group might best be called reconcilers. For the sake of church unity, reconcilers can live in a church where others think and act differently about the church's sexual ethics, same-sex marriage, and ordination standards. The new caucus group Uniting Methodists seeks to represent this faction in the church.

Those who support this position could make room for pastors who could not, in good conscience, preside at same-sex weddings *and* for pastors who would joyfully preside at them. If an annual conference voted to ordain openly gay clergy, reconcilers would welcome them *just as long as* other annual conferences were free to maintain the UM Church's position forbidding such ordinations.

Even more fundamentally, reconcilers would make room for people who believe "the practice of homosexuality is incompatible with Christian teaching," *and* for those United Methodists who believe such a statement is unbiblical, harmful, and an incitement to violence against LGBTQ+ people.

In their defense, reconcilers are not without convictions regarding these matters. They have them, and, when necessary, will act upon them. However, they believe the church is big enough and that unity is precious enough to accommodate people with diametrically opposing views. Despite decades of debate over the church's sexual ethics, fifty straight years of steady membership loss, and the recent plunge in average worship attendance, they remain convinced a healthy, vibrant, and united church could emerge from a denomination that included substantial constituencies with very different views about the interpretation of the Bible, the authority of Scripture, and church's sexual ethics.

A second group might be called liberalizers. Their ultimate goal is to dramatically liberalize the church's sexual ethics, its understanding of gender, and its teachings on marriage. Liberalizers, leaning into the Bible's demand for justice, particularly for those who have been marginalized and persecuted, maintain the church's present teachings are, at best, based on outdated biblical scholarship, and at worst, grounded in homophobia. They are committed to creating a church where LGBTQ+ people are fully included in every facet of the church's structure, including among the clergy, and where their relationships are blessed and celebrated by the church.

They could tolerate people who think differently than they do, but not at the price of limiting in any way the full rights and responsibilities of church membership and leadership to their LGBTQ+ brothers and sisters. In their preferred vision for the church, local United Methodist congregations must be prepared to receive an openly gay pastor, and United Methodist pastors must not refuse to preside at same-sex weddings solely on their belief that such weddings are contrary to Scripture and the traditions of the church catholic. Their goal is the radical transformation of the church's sexual ethics, teachings on marriage, and its ordination standards. They want to "convert" those who believe Scripture and Christian tradition support The UM Church's present standards.

The third group can justifiably be called conservatives. They want to conserve the church's present teachings because they believe they are rooted in Scripture, confirmed by centuries of church teaching, and are widely held by the majority of Christians around the world. They are happy to live in a church where all people are welcome to attend, but conservatives cannot endorse practices they deem incompatible with Christian teaching.

Unity at All Costs

As reconcilers, liberalizers, and conservatives await the work of the commission, a proposal from the Council of Bishops, and then the final decision of the delegates attending the February 2019 General Conference, all of them have their hopes and concerns.

The fondest hope of reconcilers (e.g., the caucus group Uniting Methodists, many church institutionalists, and many bishops) for the 2019 General Conference is that the delegates will adopt a plan that preserves the institution in largely its present form. Reconcilers acknowledge something must be done, but they hope it can be accomplished with a minimal amount of institutional disruption. A good number of United Methodists share their hope, but most acknowledge it is a very tall task, and some even think it an impossible one.

Prior to the 2016 General Conference, reconcilers pinned their hope on the "Third Way Plan" (sometimes referred to as the "local option") proposed by the Connectional Table, The UM Church body charged with visioning and stewardship of the church's mission. To reconcilers a "local option" seemed practical and fair, requiring compromise from both liberalizers and conservatives. For liberalizers, it made room for same-sex marriage and the ordination of openly LGBTQ+ people where locals were willing to allow for such liberalization. And for conservative clergy and annual conferences, it would not force them to violate their principles when it came to same-sex marriage and the ordination of openly gay candidates. Reconcilers were dismayed to discover that the 2016 General Conference did not support "Third Way Plan" or any "local option" that attempted to straddle the fence when it came to the church's sexual ethics, teachings on marriage, and ordination standards. In the end, reconcilers took some consolation in a narrowly approved motion that tabled any legislation having to do with the church's sexual ethics and created the Commission on a Way Forward.

However, despite the rejection of a local option approach at the 2016 General Conference, the Uniting Methodists caucus group and its institutional allies are once again rallying behind a plan with many of the same features as the Connectional Table's "Third Way."[7] Not surprisingly, ardent liberalizers and conservatives remain steadfastly opposed to such an approach. And many others find it bewildering that "Third Way" and "local option" supporters would once again champion such a plan when nearly all the delegates who attended the 2016 General Conference will be the same delegates who attend in 2019.

The LGBTQ+ community and other liberalizers still believe such plans are an insult to their constituencies. Such proposals, according to them, essentially tell LGBTQ+ people they will only be accepted where others in the church are willing to tolerate them. When a number of high-profile church leaders created the Uniting Methodists caucus group in September 2017, they effectively threw their support behind a local option approach. In short order, LGBTQ+ caucus groups swiftly and decisively condemned the group's willingness to bargain away their demand for full LGBTQ+ inclusion in an effort to preserve the institution in largely its present form.[8]

Conservatives also have criticized the Uniting Methodists' proposal as contrary to Scripture and Christian teaching, and wholly unworkable in practice. Organizations like the Africa Initiative, the Confessing Movement, Good News, and the Wesleyan Covenant Association reminded proponents of compromise plans that many evangelicals could not remain in a church where some endorsed the practice of homosexuality, celebrated same-sex weddings, and ordained openly gay clergy.[9] Evangelicals can remain in The United Methodist Church now, even though there is increasing disobedience, because the church's official position is biblical. But if the position changes to allow pastors and bishops to promote and celebrate what the conservatives believe is sinful, many evangelicals and even whole churches will feel forced to leave the denomination. Pragmatically, conservatives remain convinced that no church could survive, much less thrive, when its people are divided over such profound issues that are so deeply rooted in the interpretation of Scripture and the teachings of the church catholic.

Nevertheless, it is not uncommon to hear talk of local option plans with new metaphors to describe them: a "big tent" or "umbrella" or a "three-branch solution."

Another option that has been proposed is similar, but allows for greater distance between the different factions. It would call for the creation of two or three semiautonomous entities, one each for reconcilers, liberalizers, and conservatives. In practice, the three entities would have a wide degree of latitude with respect to core doctrinal teachings, social principles, and polity. On the other hand, they would share various ministries and resource services, and would continue to operate under a unified Council of Bishops. The three entities would jointly be called The United Methodist Church, but each entity could choose an additional name to more clearly identify and distinguish itself from the other entities.

Under such a proposal, the entities would work together in areas where there was clear and broad agreement—for example, on certain mission initiatives and in response to natural disasters. And, where willing, they would share and contribute to critical service agencies like Wespath (The United Methodist Church's pension and health benefits service). From time-to-time, perhaps once every four or five years, the leadership of the various entities would, in a way similar to the present World Methodist Council, meet together to make decisions regarding those ministries and agencies they shared in common.

Such a plan would, at least in theory, accomplish the Council of Bishop's two major goals: more or less definitively resolve the debate over the church's sexual ethics and maintain unity. The subsidiary entities would be semiautonomous, each with their own names and the right to make their own decisions regarding doctrine, polity, and social issues, but all would operate under and participate in a United Methodist Church.

The plan would have the added benefit of liberating three distinct bodies to engage in creative forms of ministry without the constraints of a current institutional structure that people across the connection believe is too costly and bureaucratic for the severe demographic challenges the church will be forced to confront in the 2020s and beyond.

However, such a plan faces serious, and perhaps even insurmountable, problems. First, the very aspects that make the plan commendable would likely lead to its undoing. It would almost certainly require constitutional amendments. That means over two-thirds of the delegates at the 2019 General Conference would need to approve of it, and then it would need to garner two-thirds of all the votes in all the annual conferences for ratification. Not only would that process be time consuming, delaying its implementation for one to two years, it would also give opponents ample opportunity to rally just 34 percent of United Methodist annual conference delegates to defeat it.

Second, the proposal seems more interested in preserving an institution than creating a united, healthy, vibrant, and mission-oriented church. The overarching institution would provide only a patina of unity, seem superfluous to many, and so, in time, it would be short-lived.

And finally, the three-branch plan would run up against some of the same criticisms liberalizers and conservatives have leveled against local option plans. Ardent LGBTQ+ advocates have little or no interest in being segregated from the rest of the church; they want the whole church to accept their plea for full inclusion in all places and at all times. And many conservatives could not be a part of a church that celebrated practices contrary to Scripture and two thousand years of church teaching.

Local option plans or plans calling for separate entities under an overarching church face major obstacles. It is unlikely they would gather the necessary support to pass at the 2019 General Conference, and even if they did, they would fall far short of their aim of keeping the church united.

Liberalizers Should Leave

A significant number of global conservatives believe they know the best way forward: liberalizers should simply leave the church. After all, the denomination has repeatedly rebuffed their attempts to liberalize its teachings, and it is likely to do so for the foreseeable future. Conservatives in this camp think this way forward can be implemented in one or two ways—amicably or legislatively, administratively, and litigiously if necessary.

Under the much-preferred amicable approach, The United Methodist Church would graciously allow all liberalizer congregations to exit the denomination with all their property and assets, and they would apply no penalty for unpaid apportionments.

However, under the more onerous legislative, administrative, and litigious plan, The United Methodist Church would close all the legislative loopholes liberalizers have exploited in the past and begin strictly enforcing church law either through administrative means or stiff, career-ending penalties. In short, this approach would call for forcing liberalizers out of the denomination if they continued to defy church teachings. It would also move against reconcilers who countenanced or abetted the defiance of liberalizers. And even if very public administrative maneuvers and church trials were required to remove defiant pastors, bishops, annual conferences, or even entire jurisdictions, some conservatives believe such an approach is the best way forward and is attainable.

These plans are siren songs for conservatives across the global connection. However, neither is likely to come to pass.

First, the idea that liberalizers will amicably leave the church is naive at best and delusional at worst. The plan fails to take liberalizers seriously. As stated above, they are not interested in creating a new denomination; they want to transform the one they are a part of. They find offers to leave, even offers to leave with all their property and assets, to be insulting, as if they are fighting for their "piece of the pie." Some conservatives like to tell themselves liberalizers do not want to leave because they know they do not have the financial resources to create their own church. This may or may not be true, but it's beside the point. When you believe you are fighting for justice, you don't surrender for property and assets. People who do that are called "sellouts," and that course of action is anathema to social justice advocates.

Second, the idea that liberalizers can be forced from the church is almost as far-fetched as their voluntarily leaving. If the events of the past several years have definitively demonstrated anything, it is that all the right laws in the church are of little avail if bishops and annual conferences are unwilling to enforce them. That is surely the case in the United States, and it will continue to be the case for years to come. The vast majority of US bishops simply have no stomach for all the bad press that would surround administrative maneuvers and church trials bent on evicting thousands of people from the denomination.

Couldn't we remove those bishops who refuse to hold trials or enforce our covenant? Possibly, but it is hard to imagine a better way to ruin the reputation of The United Methodist Church. If we ever began to "excommunicate" bishops (or pastors, churches, and annual conferences) because they care about LGBTQ+ persons— and that is how it would be reported in the press—we would be portrayed not as a warm-hearted, grace-giving church, but as a denomination that is hard-hearted and legalistic. Our ability to reach lost, broken people would be severely impacted because people would know us not by our love but by the punishment we inflict on those who fail to meet our standards.

Even if we decided to pay the cost of being seen as harsh and legalistic, it is unlikely we could pass the legislation necessary to close all the loopholes and enforce the covenant. To be sure, conservative US jurisdictional conferences will elect some conservative bishops who might strictly enforce the *Discipline*. However, reconcilers and liberalizers will elect far more of their own kind. And just as their predecessors found ways to thwart the will of General Conference, they will do the same, and they will do so even if future General Conferences manage to tighten church law and close loopholes.

Finally, we believe that neither the Commission on a Way Forward nor the Council of Bishops will endorse these plans; they are simply nonstarters. In that event, conservatives who are invested in them will have to convince the delegates at the 2019 General Conference to reject the preferred institutional plan and accept their solutions instead. That will be an uphill battle to say the least. The current crop of bishops, the church's bureaucratic and intransigent structure, and the liberalizers are not going to disappear anytime soon. In all likelihood, conservatives championing a hardline approach would have to acknowledge they are in for a fight that will last for at least another decade or more and will be played out as the church in the United States disintegrates or implodes in the 2020s.

Conservatives Should Leave

Another option would be for conservatives to leave the church. In the United States, this is unfortunately happening every day, individual by individual, family by family, and in some cases, by whole congregations. Many conservatives are as frustrated as reconcilers and liberalizers with the current state of affairs. They believe the church has reached an impasse, the differences are irreconcilable, and therefore further debate is only destructive. Some are clearly ready to leave the denomination—if the terms are acceptable. Only some conservatives think this way. Based on our observations and conversations, we believe it is now likely that the majority of US conservatives are in this camp, but the majority of conservatives in Africa, Europe, and the Philippines are not.

For many US conservatives, general church matters are not a high priority. They see little benefit in supporting several of the denomination's general boards and agencies, particularly those they regard as hostile to the church's sexual ethics, its teachings on marriage, and its ordination standards. In truth, many conservative pastors do what they can to shelter their people from the doings of US bishops and many of The UM Church's general boards and agencies. It is no secret that many conservatives have little confidence in US bishops and believe the church's bureaucracy is a drag on the denomination.

Therefore, at least some conservative pastors and congregations would be likely to leave under the following conditions: they are given title to all their property and assets, and they are immediately free of sending apportionment dollars to their annual conference and the general church.

But there are problems with this way forward too.

First, not all conservatives are invested in this option. Indeed, where conservatives are at their strongest—in Africa and the Philippines—they have yet to coalesce behind such a plan. Conservatives in the Central Conferences are not confronted with the presenting issues on a regular basis, so they are not always as exercised about them as people in the United States.

Second, even in the United States, a determined minority would likely reject, out of hand, any offer to leave. Why, they would justifiably ask, should we leave when we represent the majority of the global church, and when the church continues, at least on paper, to support sexual ethics, teachings on marriage, and ordination standards rooted in Scripture and the traditions of the church catholic? They would continue to ally with their global brothers and sisters to fight for what they think is right.

To be sure, a generous exit offer would bleed off some conservatives, but not all of them. In this scenario reconcilers and liberalizers would likely find themselves still locked in a battle with a large number of members with no interest in reconciliation or liberalization when it came to the presenting issues. In short, there would be no definitive resolution to the matters that exercise us, and therefore precious little unity.

The Messy Way Forward

Given this appraisal, it is no wonder the Council of Bishops seized on the creation of a commission to explore a possible way forward. It allowed them to pass along the task of resolving the greatest challenge The UM Church has confronted in its nearly fifty-year history— a task many believe they could have resolved by fulfilling their duty to promote and defend the church's teachings and seeing that its standards were followed. Instead, a number of bishops countenanced, abetted, and in some cases even participated in the open defiance of the church. With all due respect to our bishops, the inability or unwillingness of bishops to hold one another accountable has undermined their authority, eroded trust in them, and fostered a spirit of resignation and cynicism in many quarters of the church. The brutal membership numbers and the plummeting average worship attendance amply bear this out.

United Methodists need to disabuse themselves of the idea that the 2019 General Conference is going to produce a plan that definitively solves the debate over our sexual ethics and keeps the church united; it's not. Given all that has happened in just the past few years, the divisions are now too deep, and therefore some are bound to find any plan of unity to be a fiction at best.

Realistically speaking, for those who support unity at any price, they will have to acknowledge that their local option plans are unlikely to bring peace and unity. The battles over the church's sexual ethics, teachings on marriage, and ordination standards will rage on because liberalizers will continue to press for their ultimate goals. As more conservatives in the United States tire of the fight and follow other conservatives who have already left, reconcilers will discover they are now regarded as the obstinate conservatives unwilling to bow to every demand of the LGBTQ+ agenda. The mix will not result in unity, just more wrangling until the reconcilers either depart or completely capitulate.

And for conservatives who just want to be free of the fractious debate, they will have to accept that the way out could come at a steep price. It is possible that some on the Council of Bishops will balk at any proposal allowing conservatives to leave with all their property and assets and the immediate cessation of apportionment payments. Some bishops may not share the theological and ethical convictions of some of their more conservative-evangelical churches, but they are certainly in no rush to see them walk away with millions of dollars in property, assets, and steady streams of apportionment dollars. If they decide to invoke the denomination's trust clause, conservative congregations that just want to be free of the denomination and the incessant fighting could wind up in costly legal battles in uncertain attempts to retain their property and assets. Other mainline denominations, particularly the Episcopal Church, have demonstrated just how costly and bitter that path can be.

In light of all the various factions—old ones like Methodist Federation for Social Action and Good News and new ones like Uniting Methodists and The United Methodist Queer Clergy Caucus—and the various plans, which are often convoluted, complex, and require time-consuming and uncertain constitutional amendments for implementation, we make two observations: First, we are not united, and second, we are not better together. Statements to the effect that we are united and better together are tired and empty platitudes bishops and other leaders continue to tell us in an effort to prop up a largely faltering and failing institution.

In our opinion, there are only two ways forward. First, there is the honorable, gracious, and amicable way forward. Years ago, great statesmen of the church like Bill Hinson and Maxie Dunnam encouraged us to face the fact that we had reached an impasse. Both, in their own ways, encouraged us to free ourselves from fighting and hurting one another. They called on us to appoint wise and fair leaders who would amicably divide the institution into two or three new bodies, free to do ministry as consciences dictate. We acknowledge that such a course of action is easier said than done, but it is preferable to years of more fighting or simply finding clever ways to pretend we are united when really we are not.

Second, failing an amicable division of the church, we believe the 2019 General Conference delegates could simply vote to lift the trust clause for the next four years. This would give every local church that wanted to take it the opportunity to exit the denomination without the fear of having to litigate for property and assets in secular courts, and it would save annual conferences the huge cost of litigation as well. Congregations that wanted to stay in The United Methodist Church would not even have to consider the matter. Admittedly, in some or even many cases, the membership of local churches would be of two minds regarding whether to exit or remain. In these cases, annual conferences would first attempt mediation, and in the event mediation failed, the parties would submit to binding arbitration regarding the disposition of property and assets. In short, every effort would be made to keep annual conferences, local churches, and members from taking a church conflict into civil court. Such an approach, as we have witnessed in other mainline denominations, is costly, ultimately ruinous for the denomination, and a terrible public witness.

Again, we recognize even these proposals would not solve every matter—no plan will—but they are honest about where we are and seek ways to depart from one another as amicably and as graciously as possible.

As we have noted in previous chapters, The United Methodist Church is deeply divided on core matters, and it is clear it is deeply divided on a way forward.

CONCLUSION

If we are one church, we cannot act as if we are two. If we are two churches, we should not pretend to be one. And the truth is we are two churches. We see the inspiration and the authority of the Bible differently. We have different sexual ethics. We disagree on marriage and ordination. We understand our mission differently. We are even divided in our proclamation that Jesus Christ is *the* way and *the* truth and *the* life.

These are not small matters. And there is no "way forward" that will unite us. We conservatives are often criticized as being "uncompromising." When it comes to what we believe the Bible teaches clearly and consistently, "uncompromising" is a valid characterization. Some see that as a fault; we see it as faithfulness. Progressives, though, are just as "uncompromising." They believe they are fighting for justice. How can they accept a compromise that is unjust for the LGBTQ+ community and feel good about themselves? They can't and they won't. Some of their leaders have been more caustic in their comments about "a third way" that creates a local option than conservatives have been. They have referred to those who propose such a compromise as "institutionalists" who care more for preserving a denomination than they care about justice for marginalized people.

Even those progressives who accept a plan similar to the one proposed by Uniting Methodists will tell you that it's not a compromise that will cause them to stop their battle to change the sexual ethics of The United Methodist Church. It simply means they will have moved the church closer to their position, and they will continue to organize, legislate, and demonstrate for their views to become the official policies and practices of the church.

The truth is that even many of the leaders of Uniting Methodists, those who have referred to themselves as "centrists," also see "the local option" as a temporary means of keeping the denomination together until they can change the church's position in a thoroughly progressive direction. That means what they're proposing is not a true compromise that stops the fighting, but a strategic maneuver to maintain the institutional church until they can flip it to their point of view.

We are two churches, at least. And we should not pretend that we're one. Doing so will not solve our problems, it will not empower our mission, and it will not create real unity.

We can admit our differences without demonizing each other. Often when bishops and other leaders have written about the upcoming General Conference in February 2019, they state that our two options are either (1) keep fighting or (2) come together in love—as if those are our only two options. The *UMNS Digest* reported that the president of the Council of Bishops told the council, "If we do not work with our respective delegations, so that they have a change of heart and are open to going to the called General Conference to be at peace rather than be at war with one another, we will fail."[1] These kinds of statements are well intended, but they present our options as being at peace with each other or being in a battle. But there's a third option—one where we admit that we are two different churches and we decide that we don't want to fight any longer. We don't have to demonize each other. We don't have to have victims and villains. We don't have to have winners or losers. We don't have to "be at war." We just have to admit that we are not able to pursue our differing visions of faithfulness together and set each other free.

For many years United Methodists have been in a cage match. You may not be familiar with that term, but as a young boy I watched wrestling on TV. The most exciting match was when the ring was turned into a large cage, two wrestlers stepped inside, and the door to the cage would be locked behind them. They would do battle until one of them could no longer get up and continue the fight. Then the door to the cage would be opened and the winner would step out, bloodied, bruised, and battered. Barely able to lift his arms in victory, still he would be declared victorious.

That's where we have been as a church. We have been in a cage match, not able to stop fighting and not able to escape each other. Both sides have been bruised and battered. Our progressive friends tell us that our views and votes hurt and harm people, many of whom leave The United Methodist Church because of our beliefs. We receive letters every month from conservatives who tell us they are leaving The United Methodist Church because they can no longer stay in good conscience. Some who are leaving are young families who want to raise their children in a church that "believes in the Bible." Others are octogenarians who have been Methodists for seventy years and have decided before they die they are going to hear an Easter sermon that talks about the Resurrection as if it actually happened. And some are middle-aged but simply can no longer bear hearing more from the pulpit about "justice" for LGBTQ+ persons than they hear about Jesus dying on the cross to save sinners.

Both sides are losing good people. Both sides are being hurt. I don't want to harm anyone. I'm sure progressives don't either. I'm certain neither of us wants to hurt God's church. But that's what is happening because neither of us can compromise our deeply held beliefs. And that will continue to happen as long as we're together.

How many more years do we need to stay in this destructive cage match? To my progressive friends, I say, "You're never going to change us." Many of my conservative friends think, because the number of African delegates to General Conference is increasing, if we just keep making the language in the *Discipline* more restrictive, we will "win." To these friends I say, "At what cost? How many more good Methodists are you willing to see leave the denomination so we can 'win'? What will be left of the denomination you so want to take control of if we ever do?"

Isn't the way to win for both sides simply to stop fighting, open the door to the cage, and set each other free? That's the option so many of our leaders don't seem capable of recognizing. There is a better way than one or both sides having to compromise their principles. There is a better way than continuing the cage match where one side is defeated and the side that wins is bruised and battered. Let us stop fighting, wish each other well, and open the cage. That's not a lack of love. That's the way of love.

SELECTED READINGS

Balch, David L., ed. *Homosexuality, Science, and the "Plain Sense" of Scripture*. Grand Rapids: Eerdmans, 2000.

Boswell, John. *Christianity, Social Tolerance, and Homosexuality: Gay People in Western Europe from the Beginning of the Christian Era to the Fourteenth Century*. Chicago: University of Chicago Press, 1980.

Brooten, Bernadette. *Love Between Women: Early Christian Responses to Female Homoeroticism*. Chicago: University of Chicago Press, 1996.

Brownson, James. *Bible, Gender, Sexuality: Reframing the Church's Debate on Same-Sex Relationships*. Grand Rapids: Eerdmans, 2013.

DeYoung, Kevin. *What Does the Bible Really Teach about Homosexuality?* Wheaton, IL: Crossway, 2015.

Furnish, Victor Paul. *The Moral Teachings of Paul*. 3rd ed. Nashville: Abingdon Press, 2010.

Gagnon, Robert. *The Bible and Homosexual Practice: Texts and Hermeneutics*. Nashville: Abingdon Press, 2001.

Hays, Richard B. *The Moral Vision of the New Testament: Community, Cross, New Creation: A Contemporary Introduction to New Testament Ethics*. New York: HarperOne, 1996.

Nissinen, Martti. *Homoeroticism in the Biblical World: A Historical Perspective*. Minneapolis: Fortress, 1998.

Schmidt, Thomas. *Straight and Narrow? Compassion and Clarity in the Homosexuality Debate*. Downers Grove, IL: Intervarsity, 1995.

Soards, Marion. *Scripture and Homosexuality: Biblical Authority and the Church Today*. Louisville: Westminster John Knox, 1995.

Vines, Matthew. *God and the Gay Christian: The Biblical Case in Support of Same-Sex Relationships*. New York: Convergent, 2014.

Wold, Donald. *Out of Order: Homosexuality in the Bible and the Ancient Near East*. Grand Rapids: Baker, 1998.

NOTES

Preface

1   Readers interested in further study can consult the "Selected Readings" section in this book as well as the extensive bibliographies in those resources and the others we have cited.

2   *The Book of Discipline of The United Methodist Church, 1972* (Nashville: The United Methodist Publishing House, 1972); ¶72.C. Though the current wording is changed slightly, it is substantially the same in the equivalent paragraph of the 2016 *Book of Discipline*; ¶161.G.

3   *The Book of Discipline, 2016*; ¶161.G.

4   For more on this, see Rob Renfroe, "Three Requests of My Centrist Friends—An Open Letter," *Good News*, June 27, 2016, https://goodnewsmag.org/2016/06/three-requests-of-my-centrist-friends-an-open-letter/.

Chapter 1

1   *The Book of Discipline, 2016*; ¶120.

2   Though we do not wish to identify individuals by name here, each of these instances has been verified through the review of publicly available statements online or corroborated by several witnesses.

3   Adam Hamilton, *Making Sense of the Bible: Rediscovering the Power of Scripture Today* (New York: HarperOne, 2014), 273–274.

4   Tom Griffith, "Give a Cheer for Our Evangelical Brothers and Sisters," *Open Hands* 10, no. 3 (Winter 1995): 21.

5   Matt Smith, "A Quiet Struggle Within the Gay Marriage Fight," *The New York Times*, February 18, 2012, http://www.nytimes .com/2012/02/19/us/within-gay-marriage-battle-a-quiet-struggle -in-churches.html.

6   Bishop Scott J. Jones, e-mail message to author, December 8, 2017, confirming the bishop's statement at a 2017 district meeting that the author attended.

Chapter 2

1   Carrie Surbaugh, "An Open Letter to My Parents' Pastor," *United Methodist Insight*, July 13, 2017, http://um-insight.net /in-the-church/local-church/an-op/.

2   See Robert Wall, "Reading Scripture, the Literal Sense, and the Analogy of Faith," in *Wesley, Wesleyans, and Reading Bible as Scripture*, ed. Joel B. Green and David F. Watson (Waco: Baylor University Press, 2012).

3   *The Book of Discipline 2016*; ¶104, Article V, "Of the Sufficiency of the Holy Scriptures for Salvation."

4   See Article XX of the "Articles of Religion," http://anglicansonline .org/basics/thirty-nine_articles.html. For what seemed to him and his contemporaries to be an obvious reason, Wesley did not include this article in his amended version for the Methodist Episcopal Church. He read the article as applicable to the Church of England, and therefore it no longer had any bearing on a people completely free of its authority.

5   Joel B. Green and David F. Watson, ed., in *Wesley, Wesleyans, and Reading Bible as Scripture* (loc. 3469, Kindle).

6   John Wesley, Preface to *Sermons on Several Occasions*, paragraph 5, in *The Works of John Wesley*, Vol. 2, ed. Albert C. Outler (Nashville: Abingdon Press, 1985), 106.

7   John Wesley, "Preface to the New Testament Notes," paragraph 10, *John Wesley's Notes on the Bible*, Wesley Center Online, http://wesley.nnu.edu/john-wesley/john-wesleys-notes-on -the-bible/preface-to-the-new-testament-notes/.

8   To think more in terms of a pyramid is closer to what Wesley had in mind. Scripture is the base. Tradition, reason, and experience complete the structure, but they are predicated upon the sure

foundation of Scripture. Such a model is a valid understanding of what is outlined in The UM Church's *Discipline.*

9   William J. Abraham, "What's Right and What's Wrong with the Quadrilateral?" *Canadian Methodist Historical Society Papers* 13 (2001): 136–50.

10 Robert B. Coote and Mary P. Coote, *Power, Politics, and the Making of the Bible* (Minneapolis: Fortress, 1990), 11.

11 Ibid., 72. See also A. K. M. Adam, *What Is Postmodern Biblical Criticism?* (Minneapolis: Fortress, 1995), 54.

12 For a thorough ideological reading of the Old Testament, see Giovanni Garbini, *History and Ideology in Ancient Israel* (New York: Crossroad, 1988).

13 See the characterization of Paul in Coote and Coote, *Power, Politics, and the Making of the Bible,* 106–107.

14 See Richard Hays's essay "A Hermeneutic of Trust" in his *The Conversion of the Imagination: Paul as Interpreter of Israel's Scripture* (Grand Rapids: Eerdmans, 2005), 190–201.

15 Hamilton, *Making Sense of the Bible,* 273–274.

16 Thomas Jefferson, *The Jefferson Bible: The Life and Morals of Jesus of Nazareth* (Boston: Beacon Press, 1989). For Jefferson's harsh critique of the Gospel writers see pp. 17, 27–30 in the introduction by F. Forrester Church.

17 In a response to David Watson's critique of his buckets metaphor, Hamilton has written that he intended it to "foster a conversation among Christians." He also acknowledged that "what was missing [from his argument] was the theological foundation that leads me to speak of the three buckets, and . . . the criteria by which we determine which bucket a scripture goes in." See https: //davidfwatson.me/2014/03/16/adam-hamiltons -response-to-three-buckets-calmly-considered/.

18 Wesley, "Preface to the New Testament Notes," paragraph 10.

19 Griffith, "Give a Cheer for our Evangelical Brothers and Sisters," *21.*

20 J. Richard Peck, "Church Should Examine the Reason for Its Differences," United Methodist News Service, 2004, quoted in "Podcast: Rob Renfroe on 'The Deeper Issues of Methodist Renewal,'" (address, gathering of the Arkansas Conference Confessing Movement, June 2007), audio player, 27:42 (at 11:25 mark), November 18, 2010, *MethodistThinker.com,* https://methodistthinker.com/2010/11/18/podcast-rob-renfroe-on -the-deeper-issues-of-methodist-renewal/.

Chapter 3

1   Kathy Gilbert and Tita Parham, "Delegates Cannot Agree They Disagree on Sexuality," *UMNS Digest*, May 3, 2012, http://www .umc.org/news-and-media/delegates-cannot-agree-they-disagree -on-sexuality.

2   Heather Hahn, "Bishop Accused of Urging Disobedience," *UMNS Digest*, http://www.umc.org/news-and-media/bishop -accused-of-urging-disobedience.

3   Richard B. Hays, *The Moral Vision of the New Testament* (New York: HarperCollins, 1996), 389.

4   Ben Witherington, "Gender Matters: Human Sexuality and the Bible Yet Again" (unpublished manuscript, n.d.), Microsoft Word file.

5   A creative but absurd argument is that when Paul writes about having "unnatural relations" he is talking about men and women who have homosexual relations when they are actually heterosexual by nature. They sin against their own nature. It is laughable to be told that Paul didn't know about persons having homosexual natures the way we do now and then to argue that Paul is condemning people who do not have homosexual natures for engaging in homosexual sex. You simply cannot have it both ways. The meaning of the Greek phrase *kata physin* is explained in Witherington's "Gender Matters" as well as other sources. It has nothing to do with the individual's nature but to what is natural and right for the species.

6   Andy Coghlan, "Largest Study of Gay Brothers Homes in on 'Gay Genes.'" *New Scientist*, November 17, 2014, https://www .newscientist.com/article/dn26572-largest-study-of-gay-brothers -homes-in-on-gay-genes/.

7   Gary Greenberg, "Gay by Choice? The Science of Sexual Identity," *Mother Jones*, August 27, 2007, http://www.motherjones.com /politics/2007/08/gay-choice-science-sexual-identity/.

8   Ibid.

9   Francis Collins, *The Language of God: A Scientist Presents Evidence for Belief* (New York: Free Press, 2006), 260.

Chapter 4

1   The United Methodist Church Operational Assessment Project, Apex HG, LLC, 161–162, 216 (Call to Action), http://s3.amazonaws .com/Website_Properties/connectional-table/documents /call-to-action-operational-assessment-apex-report.pdf.

2   Sam Hodges, "Term Limits for Bishops Fails at GC 2016," *UMNS Digest*, May 17, 2016, http://www.umc.org /news-and-media/term-limits-for-bishops-fails-at-gc2016.

3   "Mixed Blessing in New U.S. Church Numbers," *UMNS Digest*, http://www.umc.org/news-and-media/mixed-blessings-in-new -us-church-numbers.

4   Walter Fenton, "Economist Crunches UM Numbers," *Good News*, April 1, 2016, https://goodnewsmag.org/2016/04/economist -crunches-um-numbers/.

5   Pete Townsend, "Won't Get Fooled Again," 1971.

6   *Outreach Magazine* identified the following Southern California churches among the top fifty in 2017: Saddleback Church, The Rock Church, Mariners Church, North Coast Church, and Shepherd Church. See "100 Largest Churches 2017," *Outreach Magazine*, http://www.outreachmagazine.com /outreach-100-largest-churches-2017.html?pag=1.

7   UCC Center for Analytics, Research and Data, "The United Church of Christ: A Statistical Profile with Reflection/Discussion Questions for Church Leaders," Fall 2016, 3. http://uccfiles.com /pdf/Fall-2016-UCC-Statistical-Profile.pdf.

8   UCC Center for Analytics, Research and Data, "Futuring the United Church of Christ: 30-Year Projections," Draft Results, June 2015, http://uccfiles.com/pdf/Projections-Handout.pdf.

9   David Goodhew, "Facing Episcopal Church Decline," *Living Church*, July 24, 2017, https://livingchurch.org /covenant/2017/07/24/facing-episcopal-church-decline/.

10 Steve Salyards, PCUSA Membership Numbers for 2016, *The Layman*, May 30, 2017, https://www.layman.org/pcusa -membership-numbers-2016/.

Chapter 5

1   Sam Hodges and Beth DiCocco, "New England Conference Votes 'Non-Conformity' with UMC's LGBTQI Policies," *United Methodist Insight*, June 20, 2016, http://um-insight.net /in-the-world/advocating-justice/new-england-conference-votes -non-conformity-with-umc-s-lgbtq/.

2   Linda Bloom, "Judicial Council Takes Up Gay Ordination Issue," *UMNS Digest*, October 17, 2016, http://www.umc .org/news-and-media/judicial-council-takes-up-gay -ordination-issue; and Linda Bloom, "Review All Clergy

Qualifications, Court Says," *UMNS Digest*, April 28, 2017, http://www.umc.org/news-and-media/review-all-clergy -qualifications-court-says.

3   "Judicial Council Releases Decisions on LGBTQ Related Items," Reconciling Ministries Network, October 29, 2017, https://rmnetwork.org/judicialcouncil2017/.

4   Walter Fenton, "Largest Congregation in Mississippi Parts Ways with UM Church," *Good News*, May 26, 2017, https://goodnewsmag.org/2017/05/largest-congregation-in -mississippi-parts-ways-with-um-church/.

5   See "Financial Crisis," https://www.yacumc.org/files/content /annual+conference/2017/yac+financial+crisis+6-10-2017.pdf.

6   Walter Fenton, "Plunge in UM Average Worship Attendance Hits New Record," *Good News*, December 9, 2016, https://goodnewsmag.org/2016/12/plunge-in-um-average -worship-attendance-hits-new-record/.

7   See "Officiation" and "Ordination" at http://unitingmethodists.com.

8   See "UMQCC Response to Uniting Methodists," September 21, 2017, http://um-insight.net/in-the-church/a-way-forward /umqcc-response-to-uniting-methodists/.

9   See "Chicago Statement to the Bishops' Commission on a Way Forward," October 7, 2017, https://wesleyancovenant.org/wca -statements-and-beliefs/#chicago.

Conclusion

1   Heather Hahn, "Bishop Called to Navigate 'Off the Map,'" *UMNS Digest*, November 6, 2017, http://www.umc.org/news-and-media /bishops-called-to-navigate-off-the-map.